EASTERN EUROPE
IN A
TIME OF CHANGE

EASTERN EUROPE
IN A
TIME OF CHANGE

Economic and Political Dimensions

Iliana Zloch-Christy

PRAEGER

Westport, Connecticut
London

HC
244
Z57
1994

Library of Congress Cataloging-in-Publication Data

Zloch-Christy, Iliana
    Eastern Europe in a time of change : economic and political
    dimensions / by Iliana Zloch-Christy.
        p.   cm.
    Includes bibliographical references and index.
    ISBN 0–275–94707–6 (alk. paper)
    1. Europe, Eastern—Economic conditions—1989– 2. Former
Soviet republics—Economic conditions. 3. Europe, Eastern—
Social conditions. 4. Former Soviet republics—Social conditions.
I. Title.
HC244.Z57   1994
338.947—dc20   93–26469

British Library Cataloguing in Publication Data is available.

Library of Congress Catalog Card Number: 93–26469
ISBN: 0–275–94707–6

First published in 1994

Praeger Publishers, 88 Post Road West, Westport, CT 06881
An imprint of Greenwood Publishing Group, Inc.

Printed in the United States of America

The paper used in this book complies with the
Permanent Paper Standard issued by the National
Information Standards Organization (Z39.48–1984).

10 9 8 7 6 5 4 3 2 1

To
Daniela

Contents

Acknowledgments

I prepared the bulk of this monograph during my research fellowship at Harvard in 1992–93, and part of it during my scholarship at the Hoover Institution on War, Revolution and Peace at Stanford University in 1991. I would like to acknowledge the stimulating intellectual atmosphere of these universities—fascinating places of knowledge and reason. I have also benefited from discussions at the seminars held in the Departments of Economics, at the J. F. Kennedy School of Government, Baker Business School, Center for International Affairs, and Russian Research Center, as well as at the Department of Economics at MIT. I am deeply grateful in particular to Professor Richard Cooper for giving me the opportunity to conduct my work at Harvard's Department of Economics. Professor William Bossert and Mrs. M. L. Bossert introduced me to the enthusiastic and tireless environment of Lowell House. I am indebted to J. Berliner, S. Rosefielde, Shirley Williams and W. Weigel for stimulating comments on an earlier version of this study. G. Bakos, W. Bienkowski, R. Cooper, D. Bond, S. Fischer, J. Galbright, M. Hakogi, M. Kaser, J. Kornai, E. Lazear, R. Staar, T. Vultchev and H. P. Widmaier have all provided helpful advice. At Stanford University's Hoover Institution I benefited from participation in the conference on "Eastern Europe in Transition" in May 1991 with K. Arrow, V. Dlohy, M. Friedman, F. P. Johnson, Jr., R. McKinnon, and Ch. Wolf, Jr. None of these people bears responsibility for the views expressed or any remaining errors in this study. My research at Harvard was partly funded with the E. Schrodinger award of the Austrian Science Foundation.

Finally, a word of gratitude to my daughter Daniela, who spent many hours with me at libraries, conferences and seminars on both sides of the Atlantic showing so much patience. To her I lovingly dedicate this study.

Lowell House, Harvard University,
Cambridge, MA, March 1993

List of Abbreviations

BIS	Bank for International Settlements
CIS	Commonwealth of Independent States
CMEA	Council for Mutual Economic Assistance
CPE	centrally planned economy
DME	developed market economies
EBRD	European Bank for Reconstruction and Development
EC	European Community
ECE	Economic Commission for Europe
EFTA	European Free Trade Association
EIB	European Investment Bank
EPS	European Payments System
EPU	European Payments Union
GATT	General Agreement on Tariffs and Trade
GDP	gross domestic product
GNP	gross national product
IBRD	International Bank for Reconstruction and Development (The World Bank)

IMF	International Monetary Fund
LDC	less developed country
LIBOR	London interbank offered rate
NIC	newly industrialized country
NMP	Net Material Product
OECD	Organization for Economic Cooperation and Development
OPEC	Organization of Petroleum Exporting Countries
UN	United Nations
UNCTAD	United Nations Conference on Trade and Development

Introduction

Democracy extends the sphere of individual freedom, socialism restricts it. Democracy attaches all possible value to each
man; socialism makes each man a mere agent, a mere
number. Democracy and socialism have nothing in common
but one word: equality. But notice the difference: while
democracy seeks equality in liberty, socialism seeks equality
in restraint and servitude.

Alexis de Tocqueville, 1848

The most dangerous time for an authoritarian regime is when
it begins to reform itself.

Alexis de Tocqueville

Man is free if he needs to obey no person but solely the laws.

Voltaire

Among the most compelling issues of contemporary world politics
are the changes taking place in postcommunist Europe. Many
fellow economists for whom the centrally planned economies were
a subject with no real interesting problems before 1989 are now
vitally engaged in analyzing the processes of economic and
political transition. For those of us who are both professionally and

emotionally attached to Eastern Europe[1] and have experienced the totalitarian political system in this region at first hand, it is a time for profound thought and studied action. The political and economic transformation of Eastern Europe and the former Soviet Union, now the Commonwealth of Independent States (CIS), in the 1990s represents by far one of the most important events in postwar world politics. The Central and Eastern Europe of the mid-1990s will be quite different from the Soviet-dominated region of the mid-1980s.[2]

Even the most conservative observers agree that the process toward democratization and economic restructuring in Eastern Europe is irreversible. Only a few years ago Russian participation in the economic summits of the Group of Seven and membership in the international Bretton Woods institutions (the International Monetary Fund and the World Bank) would have been inconceivable and merely an optimistic goal of a distant future. But the reality proved this expectation to be wrong. Other unexpected realities are the unification of Germany and the formation of noncommunist governments first in Poland in 1989 and then in Hungary and the former Czechoslovakia. In addition, the influence of the noncommunist opposition (stemming formally not from the Communist party or from the renamed Communist party, now usually called the "Socialist" party) has increased in the Parliament of Bulgaria, and in late 1991 a noncommunist government was formed there and stayed in power until December 1992. The political landscape in Romania is still unclear, although there are certain signs of retreat from the authoritarian Ceausescu-style policies; this relaxation is also evident in a number of former Soviet republics and particularly in the Asian republics.

To understand the economic problems of the former Soviet Union and Eastern Europe, we must conduct a complex analysis of the many economic, social, political, nationality and ethnic issues of transformation. The ancient Chinese greeting, "May you live in interesting times," obviously has great relevance for the economists and other social scientists engaged in the field of Eastern European studies. But at the same time the complexity of the problems and the rapidly unfolding events in this region make it extremely difficult for politicians and scholars alike to analyze the process and to attempt any predictions. In this connection, we might mention the introductory remarks which the well-known student of socialist economics Janos Kornai chose for his recent book on socialist economics and political economy (1992, p. xix). He quotes Chou En-lai's comments on the significance of the French Revolution: "It is too early to say." This thought applies equally well to our study of present-day developments in Eastern Europe. It is too early for academics to provide a comprehensive scholarly analysis, and it is too early for politicians to comment on this great event.[3] Most scholars and politicians do agree on one point, however: the ongoing changes in postcommunist Europe are *revolutionary*; that is, they are revolutions from above, or, as Zbigniew Brzezinski has put it, "political liberalization with economic retrogression is a classic formula for revolution."[4]

A few years ago in our study of the so-called socialist economies (centrally planned economies), as Professor Kornai expressed it, "most of us dealing with the subject [had] only conjectures and hypotheses."[5] Today the study of post-Soviet and Eastern European economics faces new challenges, with the primary question being how to transform a planned economy into a market economy. Scholars and politicians in both the East and West continue, unavoidably, to deal with conjectures and hypotheses on this matter of transformation. The two principal questions that they pose are the scientific-technical question "What can be done?" and the ethical-political question "What should be done?" The answers to these questions involve not only economic theory but also political economy and politics. Obviously, politics in the process of economic transformation in postcommunist Europe is not an "externality" factor. The new political economists view political variables as endogenous.[6] While this issue is beyond the scope of the present study, I would like only to point out that the relationship between political economy and politics is more complex than that. Political economy of necessity encroaches on politics, inasmuch as government intervenes and presents its economic policy through its political platform.

The ongoing economic transformation has been accompanied by changes in all spheres of Eastern European societies. The political challenge for this region is to make these changes as smoothly and painlessly as possible. More than fifty years ago John Maynard Keynes addressed this problem of change: "The political problem of mankind is to combine three things: Economic Efficiency, Social Justice and Individual Liberty" (1963, p. 344). It is this question that Eastern Europe must face as it undertakes its Herculean economic and political task in the 1990s.

The Czech economist and politician Vaclav Klaus states that his country is attempting to "create a normally functioning market economy and a normally functioning political system based on standard political parties" (1992, p. 73). The same sentiment can be heard in the statements of politicians from the other Eastern European countries as well. But theory cannot definitively reveal the "best and safe road in getting to market" for Russia and the former Soviet republics and Eastern Europe. In both the nineteenth and twentieth centuries, many economists and political scientists focused on the capitalist economies and on the question of how to convert market economies into socialist planned systems. Among these analysts were the Cambridge economist Joan Robinson, the Polish economist Oscar Lange, and the Russian-American economist Wassily Leontieff. In the last several decades the most prominent economists of our time, Ludwig von Mises, Friedrich von Hayek, Milton Friedman and Joseph Schumpeter, although from different schools of thought, pointed to the errors made by socialist advocates. But comprehensive studies dealing with the problems of transformation from command to market economies are still in scant supply.

As Paul Samuelson notes, even as economics became more "scientific" it never lost its interest in policy (1989, p. 827). Many economists of our time, though convinced of the need for fundamental changes in the established regimes, insist that plans for alternative economic systems be practical. In this respect, the interdependence of economic and political changes becomes an issue of great importance in analyzing developments in the former Soviet Union and Eastern Europe.

How will democratization affect the economic transformation? How will changes in economic behavior and mechanisms influence the political transformation? What are the alternative scenarios for economic development strategies and for political developments in the short and medium term? These are the principal questions I address in this study. By attempting to answer these questions, I hope ultimately to provide an analytical framework through which we can evaluate the postcommunist European economies and societies with a primary focus on economic perspectives.

The structure of this study is as follows. Chapter 1 explores the basic changes in the economic and political life of Eastern Europe after 1989; Chapter 2 examines the ongoing economic transformation; Chapter 3 turns specifically to a brief analysis of the relationship between economic reform and political changes in the postcommunist Europe; Chapter 4 studies possible economic development strategies during the 1990s; and Chapter 5 discusses one of the main issues of the economic reform—currency convertibility. The main findings are presented in the Conclusion.

The first draft of the study was completed in 1991 and is a continuation of my previous studies on the economic developments and the external balance of Eastern Europe (Zloch-Christy, 1988, 1991). In the first two years after the revolutions of 1989, we the students of Soviet and Eastern European economics had an opportunity to clarify our initial ideas about the transformation. For many scholars and politicians it was a time of great expectations and hopes for rapid changes in the region. Economic and political developments in Eastern Europe are so diverse and complex, however, that a detailed discussion of these processes is almost impossible. Such a discussion is not, of course, the goal of my present work. While I have made revisions of my studies in 1992 and in February 1993, the cautiously optimistic conclusions of my book still stand.

EASTERN EUROPE
IN A
TIME OF CHANGE

1

Eastern Europe on a Road Toward Radical Change

The former Soviet Union and the postcommunist Central and Eastern European countries today have a historical opportunity to adopt democracy and to achieve an efficient market economy that may help lead their populations to material wealth. They also have a historical opportunity to catch up with the western part of Europe which attained great economic success and stable democracies after the Second World War. Western Europe is considered one of the most dynamic economic areas in the world, and the European Community's integration plans promise even more spectacular economic gains in the future. As is well known democratization and the market economy involve decentralization, devolution and competition. *Democracy* decentralizes and devolves political power among competing parties, groups, candidates and voters, whereas the *market economic order* decentralizes and devolves economic power among competing producers and competing consumers.

SOME HISTORICAL CONSIDERATIONS

The Eastern European countries achieved a modest record of democratic order and market economy before World War II. The dominant orders for 100 years in this region, until 1989, were feudalism, fascism and communism. But to understand their on-going transformation, we must consider not just the previous four decades of communist rule and centralized economy, but also their earlier history, political culture and political structures, as well as their means of exercising power, particularly in the interwar period. These issues are not within the direct province of the present study,[1] but we should stress here the general traditions of the countries in question. Tsarist Russia, for example, while under its long authoritarian rule, had a very weak form of capitalism and an incompetent and corrupt bureaucracy. A. Gerschenkorn contends that even without the events of 1917 capitalism would have developed only slowly in Russia because of its inefficient banking system (relative, for example, to the systems in Great Britain and the United States) which reflected the corruption of its society. Bourgeois democracy had a very short reign in Russia in 1917 and was followed by the so-called proletarian revolution.

In Eastern Europe multiparty societies developed in the interwar period, particularly in the 1920s. Economic and political developments in these countries were greatly influenced by the economic and political philosophy of the European Great Powers, namely, Germany, Great Britain and France.[2] Their governments, however, were unstable, changing with great frequency, especially in Poland. After the Great Depression, authoritarian rule was introduced not only in Germany, Italy and Spain, but also in Eastern Europe. In Eastern Europe this development promoted the demise of democratic institutions and an explosion of nationalistic passions. Among the authoritarian regimes of the 1930s were those led by General Pilsudski in Poland, Admiral Horthy in Hungary, Tiso in Slovakia, the Iron Guard in Romania and the "Nineteenth of May" (1934) military government in Bulgaria. The only exceptions to this general development in Eastern Europe were the Czech lands where democracy succeeded while failing elsewhere in the region. As Sharon Wolchik points out, the Czech lands had "the best preconditions for creating and sustaining democratic government."[3]

Only in the Czech lands, as well as in Hungary and in the south of Poland, did the citizenry have traditions of autonomous, pluralistic group activity and some record of limited self-government attained earlier under the relatively liberal Austrian rule during the Austro-Hungarian empire. (In contrast, other parts of Eastern Europe had been under the more authoritarian Russian and Prussian rule.) As a result, in combination with other factors (see note 3) the Czech lands had a better climate for democracy in the 1930s.

RADICAL TRANSFORMATION

The present-day transformation process in Eastern Europe is one of instability and unpredictability, marked by the individual countries' growing pains and difficulties in readjustment from the recent economic period to the new one. Nonetheless, this process has its own dynamic and political logic,[4] based on the interaction among various economic, social and political changes.

How are we to explain these processes and the possible directions of future economic and political developments? To answer this extremely difficult question, we can profitably recall Ockham's Razor, a principle named after an English cleric of the fourteenth century. According to this principle, simple explanations and answers are to be preferred to complex ones, and complexities should be introduced only when simple explanations prove inadequate. Though initially proposed as a guide to philosophic inquiry, this concept can also be helpful in the nonphilosophical realms.

Let me begin my analysis with a statement by one of the most prominent economists of our century Joseph Schumpeter in his study *Capitalism, Socialism and Democracy* (1942):

Can capitalism survive? No. I do not think it can. But this opinion of mine, like that of every other economist who has pronounced upon the subject, is in itself completely uninteresting. What counts in any attempt at social prognosis is not the Yes or No that sums up the facts and arguments which lead up to it but these facts and arguments themselves.

They contain all that is scientific in the final result. Everything else is not science but prophecy. Analysis, whether economic or other, never yields more than a statement about tendencies present in an observable pattern. And these never tell us what will *happen* to the pattern but only what *would* happen if they continued to act as they have been acting in the time interval covered by our observation and if no other factors intruded. "Inevitability" or "necessity" can never mean more than this (p. 61).

This statement is an indictment of capitalism, which since the Industrial Revolution has been plagued by crisis, inequality and depressions. Capitalism's critics increased after the Second World War, and again Schumpeter was the economist who was stressing that capitalism, while economically stable and even gaining in stability, would be changed (not by economic necessity) into an order of things which only a matter of taste and terminology would determine whether or not it would be called socialism.[5]

These remarks are a persuasive reflection of the eternal search for visions of a more perfect society. This search has always fascinated philosophers: Plato's Republic, Sir Thomas More's Utopia and Marx's dictatorship of the proletariat have, over the ages, been among the most influential of these visions. As for the dictatorship of the proletariat, after more than seventy years of reality in the Soviet Union and more than forty years in Central and Eastern Europe, it proved to be a doctrine legalizing one of the most oppressive political regimes in history. Its economic and political mechanism and policies were indisputable failures, and, in hindsight, it was clearly only a matter of time before the economic system it maintained would break down. The well-known Soviet dissident Yuri F. Orlov describes this problem in relation to the former Soviet Union:

Gorbachev understood nothing when he began. . . . All he knew was that socialism must be improved. His idea was simple, and close to Western thinking: if you take socialism and add democracy and free speech, all will be well. But what he discovered was that the system designed by Lenin was such that once you pulled out one brick, the whole thing fell apart. Now he's trying to push the brick back in. This is the farce and the tragedy (cited in Kornai, 1992, p. 571, as originally reported in the *New York Times*, 10 February 1991, p. 4).

The economists Keynes, von Mises and Hayek, though from two different schools of thought, were among the first to foresee the failure of central planning. During the first decades of the Soviet state Keynes wrote: "How can I accept a doctrine which sets up as its bible, above and beyond criticism, an obsolete economic textbook which I know to be not only scientifically erroneous but without interest or application for the modern world" (1963, p. 300). Ludwig von Mises argued in his book *Socialism*, published in Vienna in 1922, that rational economic calculation would be impossible under communism. Hayek (1946) expressed it differently:

The clash between planning and democracy arises simply from the fact that the latter is an obstacle to the suppression of freedom which the direction of economic activity requires (p. 38). . . . The nightmare of English nineteenth-century political thinkers: the state in which as Disraeli expressed it, "no avenue to wealth and honour would exist save through the government" would be realised in a completeness which they never imagined—though familiar enough in some countries which have since passed to totalitarianism (p. 56). . . . Economic power centralised as an instrument of political power creates a degree of dependence scarcely distinguishable from slavery (p. 71).

But we can go back even further than Keynes and Hayek to more than a century ago when John Stuart Mill wrote:

A fixed rule like that of equality, might be acquiesced in, and so might chance, or an external necessity; but that a handful of human beings should weigh everybody in the balance, and give more to one and less to another at their sole pleasure and judgement, would not be borne unless from persons believed to be more than men, and backed by supernatural terrors (cited in Hayek, 1946, p. 59).

Although the market economies (or, more accurately, the mixed economies) of the United States, Western Europe and Japan formed a common pattern of unprecedented rapid growth and expanding international trade, the critics of capitalism increased in numbers in the 1970s and 1980s when inflation soared, unemployment rose, government deficits began to climb, the international financial system faced the danger of massive defaults on the debt incurred by the less developed countries, and the environment posed alarming demands. Even the smaller welfare states in Western Europe like Sweden (with its famous Swedish economic model), Norway and Austria, after experiencing stable economic growth in the previous two decades, now faced the problems of a sluggish economy. Specifically, they now had to overcome government revenues, rapidly rising expenditures, a tremendous explosion in deficits (ranging from some 10 to 14 percent of the gross national product), inflationary pressures and unemployment.[6]

Economists in the West have again been challenged to find better ways for the government to help (or at least stop hindering) economic development.[7] The Western economies have problems, and the diagnosis points to a state of illness. Critics from both left and right are searching for policies and schemes that will *revive* the economies in the West.

The state of affairs in the Commonwealth of Independent States and in Eastern Europe is *fundamentally different*. Scholars and politicians in both the East and West agree that there are no "medicines" that can revive the former centrally planned economies in the region. Their sickness is incurable, and the only way to avoid a protracted crisis in the long term is to transform the economic mechanism.

TRANSFORMATION TOWARD A WESTERN-TYPE MARKET

The rhetoric about transformation in Eastern Europe often employs the term *market*. Accordingly, a brief description of the concept of market would be appropriate here. Market, as a discovery process and as a form of social cooperation arising from unforced interactions between individuals, could be defined as an exchange of commodities and services, but this brief definition needs several important additions and clarifications. To begin with, we can cite John Hicks's opinion: "The merchant must have property in the things in which he trades; his right to that property must be identifiable" (1986 [1969], p. 34). Further important features of the market are voluntary exchange, horizontal rather than vertical economic links, no monopolization, competition (including international agents), a unified tax system offering more or less equal conditions for the economic agents, (effective) monetary policy,[8] private ownership and guaranteed property rights, rules of civil law, a banking system of independent central banks and competing commercial and investment banks, and commodity and capital markets. In an increasingly interdependent world and international competition, other important features of a market economy include a liberalized foreign trade system, a unified exchange rate and currency convertibility (at least on the current account) and a sophisticated custom system.[9] This list, though not exhaustive, points to four *main* characteristics of the market:[10]

- Freedom of exchange
- Freedom of competition
- Private property rights
- Economic polycentrism (deconcentration of economic power—legal and extralegal—between firms and families)

All of the previous and frequent attempts in the 1950s, 1960s and 1970s to "reform" the centrally planned economic systems in Eastern Europe were failures essentially because no attempt was made to change the *logic* of the Eastern European economic systems. In addition, no attempt was made to change the political climate for economic reform. In this regard, the Soviet economist A. Aganbegyan, in answer to the question as to why economic reforms are needed in the Soviet Union, observed: "The old economic structure, the old patterns of development, did not correspond to the new conditions both inside the Soviet Union and internationally. . . . It became very clear that it was insufficient to make minor changes in the running of the economy. New radical reform—a 'restructuring'—was needed" (Aganbegyan, 1988, p. 41).

In the late 1980s, however, not only Aganbegyan, but also most of the Soviet reform-oriented economists had not given up on the idea of preserving the centrally planned economic model. They believed that the "radical restructuring" was to be oriented mainly toward modernizing industry and introducing some "market-like" elements (incentives, prices, quasi-private ownership and others). There was, for example, no goal for large-scale privatization. In other words, the economic reforms of the late 1980s were not a radical vision for market-oriented reform. Such visions (and actions) were clearly defined in the Yeltsin/Gaidar economic reform, which is discussed in Chapter 2. (In December 1992 the new Russian government stated that this reform would remain as a platform for the transformation.) Of some relevance in this regard is the so-called Plan for Transition to the Market or the "Shatalin 500 Days Plan" (which for a variety of political reasons, mainly resistance from the KGB and the bureaucrats, never produced a government program for action). The introduction to this plan is entitled "Man, Freedom, the Market" and states that economic mistakes had brought the country to the brink of collapse and had provoked a profound crisis. It stressed that the goal of the economic transformation should be a move toward a market-oriented economy, since "mankind has not managed to create a thing more efficient than a market economy" (cited in Fischer, 1992, p. 28). Compared to Aganbegyan's, this view represents a radical change in the thinking of the reform-oriented economists in Russia and the former Soviet Union.

The rest of Eastern Europe has also been leery of radical change. The Czech Klaus, for example, states: "We have no wish to undertake new social experiments. We have had enough of such experiments in the past" (1992, p. 73). However, the enormous problems of the economic transformation, together with the associated political and social difficulties, have created social tensions and discontent in Eastern Europe, but these developments will not likely stop or reverse the ongoing radical changes, which obviously will be carried out at different rates in the individual countries. Accordingly, values, attitudes and opinions will also change at different speeds, and new civil societies will be created in postcommunist Europe. The dynamic of the economic and political processes and the legacy of the elites who took power will vary in these countries.

While for convenience the term *transformation* is used in the present study, a more precise description should involve other terms as well: *transplacement* (that is, all forces in the country working together, as in Poland, the Czech republic and the Ukraine), *replacement* (that is, forcefully imposed changes, as East Germany taking over the West German model, but not at present in the other former communist states—in the future, for example, Russian neocolonial influence may be exerted over some of the former Soviet republics); and *transformation* (that is, the former communist elites radically but peacefully changing their policies, as in Bulgaria, Hungary and, at some point, Romania). For *all* of Eastern Europe, however, three fundamental changes[11] will take place in the 1990s:

1. Short-term changes, associated with the adjustment of economic policies and the application of market-oriented policies in order to solve the macroeconomic imbalances of the (former) centrally planned economies.
2. Long-term (structural and institutional) changes, associated with the destruction of the centrally planned economic mechanism and creating the foundations of market economies.
3. Changes in international economic relations associated with the decades of "closed economy" policies even during the period of détente in the 1970s and Gorbachev's policies in the region after 1985.

In summary, the economies of the former Soviet Union and Central and Eastern Europe are in the process of transformation and will be changed *by economic necessity*. To paraphrase Schumpeter (1942, p. 61), these economies will be changed into an order of things that only a matter of taste and terminology will determine whether the system should be called capitalism or a market economy. But it is obvious that it will not be called socialism.

ALTERNATIVE ECONOMIC SYSTEMS

What are the alternative economic systems for this region of the world? Guided by the Ockham's Razor principle, I can approach this question by examining the existing economic systems in our time. First, however, let me briefly define the notion of economic system. Economic systems can be broadly defined as a network of institutions and arrangements directed toward using the scarce resources of a certain organization. They differ among themselves in the following ways: basic values (e.g., individualism, pluralism versus communalism), possible cultural-historical predisposing factors (e.g., "rules of the game") and sociology, politics, legal framework, economic foundations (e.g., private ownership versus public ownership of the means of production).[12] According to Samuelson's definition, the economic system is a

network of relations and organizations that sets the laws and regulations that govern economic activity; determines the property rights and ownership of factors of production; distributes the decision making power over production and consumption; determines the incentives motivating the different decision makers; and at the end determines *what* gets produced, *how* it gets produced, and *for whom* the output is produced (1989, p. 833).

As we observe, the way the countries of Western Europe, North Africa, Latin America, Africa and Asia organize their economies varies greatly. But one fundamental theme dominates the approach to the economic system and economic reform: how the economy responds to the basic questions of economic life—*what, how* and *for whom.* Should the economy rely primarily on government commands and intervent'cn or on the market? There are two extreme viewpoints here: anarchists and absolute communists. The first believe in the elimination of all government, and the second advocate a government operating a totalitarian, collectivized economic order in which all decisions are made by the state. In between these extremes according to Samuelson (1989, p. 833) are the following four principal economic systems: market economy, Marxism, Soviet communism and socialism.[13] These four economic systems can be briefly characterized by the following main features. The *market economy*, in its pure form, is found in laissez-faire capitalism in nineteenth-century Britain and in the United States. *Marxism* influenced the state planners in Eastern Europe, Africa and Asia with its ideas for transforming the capitalist society into socialism succeeded by communism. *Soviet communism* in the period after 1917, and one may say until 1991, advocated state ownership of all the land and most of the capital, setting wages and most prices, and central directing the macroeconomic operation of the domestic economy. *Socialism,* or *Social democratic economic order* in its twentieth-century model in Western Europe (social democratic states), proclaims democratic governments and an expanded welfare state, nationalized industries and planning of the economy (in the sense of Keynesian-style policies, although the so-called liberal socialists in many of these countries espouse pragmatic neoclassical policies and privatization at present). In other words, these are economies and societies based on constitutional democracy, markets and a welfare state.[14]

2

Economic Transformation in Eastern Europe and the Former Soviet Union

Where do the CIS and its former alliance states in Central and Eastern Europe stand now, and where will their programs[1] for making economic reforms and liberalizing the domestic economy take them? Here I will discuss the main trends in the process of economic transformation.[2]

PRINCIPAL GOALS OF THE ECONOMIC REFORMS

Although transformation in Eastern Europe is being accompanied by complicated and vaguely defined developments in the region, scholars have reached a consensus that the main pillars of the transformation and liberalization process can now be identified:

1. Privatization (to a certain point) of the means of production, and diversification of the forms of economic activity.
2. Decentralization of management decision making in the economy.
3. A return, on the political level, to the post–World War II European tradition of civil societies, reducing and eliminating the political monopoly of the single party and creating political liberalization— openness, democratic rights and multiparty societies.

Klaus, speaking of the privatization process, states that "we know that massive, rapid, large scale privatization is absolutely necessary. We know that it is not possible to do everything necessary to create a full-fledged market economy without privatization" (1992, pp. 73–74). The same idea was also stressed in public statements made by other Eastern European reformers. However, as will be discussed in Chapter 3, politicians and scholars in the individual countries are not in agreement on the speed of the privatization process and in particular the privatization of medium- and large-scale enterprises.

The terms *self-dependence*, *self-financing* and *self-management* characterize the main directions of the decentralized decision-making process in Eastern Europe. The present reforms and all the previous so-called reforms differ in two major ways. First, the Eastern European policymakers stress that economic reform will not succeed without political reform; therefore, the two reforms must be carried out simultaneously. They also stress that the former Eastern European command economies must be restructured from top to bottom. The second major difference between the previous reforms and Gorbachev's *perestroika* policy in the late 1980s and the ongoing reform is that the main pillars of the economic changes discussed above are being carried out at different speeds and through many difficulties in the individual countries. The Gorbachev policies did not have a de facto effect on the domestic economies; rather, they remained only as reform goals on paper.

Three basic, related but distinctive goals of the economic transformation on the macro- and microeconomic level are as follows:

1. To establish new legal institutions, including a new constitution, private property, law of contract and elimination of the state monopoly on international trade.
2. To achieve financial stabilization.
3. To complete a structural transformation, including the reallocation of resources, privatization and demonopolization.

The macro- and microeconomic reforms in the individual Eastern European countries also envisage the following objectives:

1. Stabilization of the economy (reducing budget deficits, anti-inflationary policy, stabilization of the external balance—debt management, export promotion, etc.).
2. Market- and price reform (e.g., liberalizing prices, cutting subsidies, tax reform—new tax administration and tax policy—creating labor and capital markets).
3. Enterprise reform (restructuring domestic industries, privatization, restructuring individual enterprises).
4. New role of the state in the economy (e.g., tax laws, tax administrations, including tax-collecting agencies, new laws and regulations for foreign investments).

The Eastern European countries and their economies represent a delicately balanced web of interests and social strata. The economic reforms require fundamental changes in the general management and macroeconomic system, and considerable shifts in resource allocation are required at the sectoral, branch and regional levels and in income policy—all of which involves a long and difficult process. Real reform changes can be briefly summarized as follows: destroying the system of central planning, quasi-liberalizing prices, creating new commercial banks (to evaluate projects and promote private business), privatizing agriculture (despite strong resistance from the *nomenklatura*) and helping the emergence of small businesses and of new human capital (new entrepreneurs, private firms, farms, etc.).[3]

The economic and political developments of 1990–93 lead to the (probably premature) conclusion that the Eastern European economies are mixed economies at present, or as Rudiger Dornbusch[4] has put it, have adopted "capitalism without profit and socialism without planning" (1992, conversation with author).

"BIG BANG" OR GRADUALISM?

All the countries in the region are confronted with the dilemma of choosing the necessary reform steps to begin with and, then, the major starting point. In 1991 and early 1992, two policy alternatives began to be discussed: first, the *big bang* (or shock therapy) approach for rapid reform changes, associated with immediate removal of existing distortions, and, second, the *gradualist* approach.

The "big bang" reform was first introduced in Poland in 1990, and its reform package was described by the then leading reform economist and finance minister L. Balcerowicz in a public lecture at Harvard University in March 1992. The package involved radical *stabilization* (tight fiscal and monetary policy, cuts in subsidies and anti-inflationary program), *liberalization* (currency convertibility, a unified exchange rate, price and trade liberalization) and *privatization* (small and medium-large firms mainly in retail trade and services). The gradualist approach, or the gradualism in the reform process, advocates carrying out structural and macroeconomic reforms gradually, thereby bringing the distorted equilibrium of the pre-reform era to the desired post-reform equilibrium or, more accurately, quasi-equilibrium. The defenders of such policies argue that the big bang approach can be associated with the old wise principle that "haste makes waste."

Obviously, no one can predict what success (or even failure) will be achieved in implementing the first or the second set of policies. The answer to the question "What to do" and "When" can be answered in various ways, and none of them is clear ex-ante. As we know from the experience of developing countries, hyperinflation and high inflation can be "treated" successfully at the inflation stabilization stage by using the "cold turkey" approach and (shock therapy) policies. These policies immediately remove existing distortions in the economy. This macroeconomic strategy proved correct in the 1980s in Bolivia, Mexico and Israel.

Poland introduced its "big bang" reform in 1990, and a year later in 1991, Czechoslovakia, Bulgaria and Romania did the same, although these three countries were not experiencing hyper- and high inflationary situations (e.g., three-digit annual inflation rates). Hungary adopted a more gradualist approach associated with the political program of its prime minister Jozsef Antal. Hungary was able to defend its policies in discussions with the international financial institutions, because, unlike the other countries of the region, it had opened up the economy and made structural changes (although with "ups" and "downs") more than twenty years before.[5]

Russia adopted "big bang" macroeconomic stabilization policies on 2 January 1992, when it liberalized prices, cut subsidies, tightened monetary policies, adopted the value-added tax and limited convertibility on the current account.[6] The other Soviet republics, in self-defense, decontrolled prices.[7] It was obvious in Russia that decisive steps had to be taken. In late 1990 in a report to the Supreme Soviets, the Russian economists Leonid Abalkin and Stanislav Shatalin wrote: "The economy is in an extremely dangerous zone—the old administrative management system has been destroyed, but the new incentives for work in market conditions have not yet been created" (cited in Fischer, 1992, p. 32).

The big bang approach as introduced in Russia and the other Eastern European countries has been accompanied, of course, by high social costs and political tensions. A February 1992 report of the Russian Academy of National Economy and Geonomics Institute in Moscow forecast that in 1992 production was likely to drop by 30 percent and investment by 50 percent; unemployment could reach 10 to 15 percent and the monthly inflation 50 to 100 percent; economic conflicts and "trade wars" between the former Soviet republics were predicted as highly probable; and the inflow of foreign investments because of the unstable economic and political situation was likely to be very small. Unfortunately, these pessimistic predictions proved to be quite true. Table A.1 shows, for example, that the decline of output in Russia in 1992 was −28 percent as compared to its level in 1989 (= 100 percent); the decline in the other large former Soviet republic, the Ukraine, was almost at the same level: −29 percent. Russia and the other former Soviet repub-

lics have been hampered by hyperinflation since 1992 and, associated with that, capital flight, dollarization of the economy and
barter transactions. Keynes described this kind of macroeconomic
situation more than seventy years ago:

If a man is compelled to exchange the fruits of his labors for paper which,
as experience soon teaches him, he cannot use to purchase what he
requires at a price comparable to that which he has received for his own
products, he will keep his produce for himself, dispose of it to his friends
and neighbors as a favor, or relax his efforts in producing it. A system of
compelling the exchange of commodities at what is not their real relative
value not only relaxes production, but leads finally to waste and inefficiency of barter. (1919 [1988], p. 236).

Many Russian and other former Soviet economists are pessimistic about the present stage of the economic reform. For example,
at his public lecture at Harvard University in November 1992 the
Russian economist N. Shmelev characterized the economic situation in Russia and in the other former Soviet republics as "highly
dangerous" from the political perspective in the long run. Some
young Russian economists even predict that social and economic
tensions in the CIS could lead to civil war.[8] It is, of course, difficult
to speculate on the consequences of the ongoing transformation in
the former Soviet Union. While it is hazardous to guess, civil war
will not be a probable scenario in the 1990s in the short term,
because at present in Russia and in the other republics no one of
the parties is strong enough to begin a war and to claim victory.
However, local ethnic and nationalistic conflicts remain a very
possible scenario in the former Soviet Union in the 1990s.

MACROECONOMIC DILEMMAS

What can be expected in the first half of the 1990s, the period
of the economic transformation in Eastern Europe? Will the self-
regulating order of the market mechanism be achieved soon? What

are the prospects for an economic order where "government governs best which governs least"?

One serious macroeconomic problem in Eastern Europe is the *tension in the external balance* of the region. The external debt situation of the Eastern European countries rapidly deteriorated in the late 1980s. The large external imbalances and the "tax on GNP" to be paid abroad represent serious macroeconomic constraints on the process of economic and political transformation. As Tables A.2 and A.3 show, the total gross and net debt of the region can be estimated at the level of some U.S.$176 billion and U.S.$154 billion, respectively, in 1992. The most heavily indebted countries are the former Soviet Union, Poland and Hungary. Bulgaria experienced serious debt-servicing difficulties in early 1990, and further reschedulings of its debt are unavoidable. The debt-service ratios (all interest and amortization on medium- and long-term debt as a percentage of one year's exports) reached alarming levels in the former Soviet Union, in Bulgaria, Poland and Hungary in 1992: 85 percent, 77 percent, 71 percent and 65 percent respectively (with 25 percent considered a critical level in business circles). In Poland, for example, servicing the accumulated external and domestic debt (capital and interest) requires some 12 percent of GNP, which is obviously a very high percentage and poses a serious burden to meet the IMF targets for budget deficits—not exceeding 5 percent (*Financial Times*, 10 March 1993, p. 3).

The former Soviet Union began to accumulate large arrears to banks and suppliers in 1990 when it requested a formal debt rescheduling with official and commercial bank creditors. Given the economic chaos in this region and the trade collapse, a further increase in debt levels will unavoidably occur in the next few years, as will refinancing some of the debt repayment that will come due. Russia itself, for example, is more than U.S.$400 million in default on U.S.$4 billion in loans of U.S. grain exports. Difficult negotiations took place in early 1993, with no clear solution achieved (*The Wall Street Journal*, 5 March 1993). According to some estimates, the combined current account deficit of the fifteen former Soviet republics will increase from U.S.$15 billion in 1992 to U.S.$20 billion at the end of 1993 (IMF, World Economic Outlook, October 1992, p. 20). The IMF, IBRD and EBRD are increasing their exposures to Eastern Europe and the former Soviet republics, with a focus on policy loans (including privatization) and stabilization of the external balance. However, in the period 1992–93 several countries in the region did not receive IMF financing, because they failed to meet negotiated budgetary and other commitments. Among these countries were Russia, the Ukraine, Poland, Hungary, Slovakia, Bulgaria and the Czech republic. EBRD financing has been rather modest, given the capacity of this relatively new financial institution.

The creditors' and debtors' policy strategies for dealing with the present situation are as follows: Interest arrears continue to hamper a normalization of creditor-debtor relations (in the former Soviet Union, Poland and Bulgaria); commercial banks stand ready on a case-by-case basis to discuss commercially viable debt buy-back agreements (e.g., the January 1993 negotiations of Russia with Austrian commercial banks), or other forms of debt and debt-service reduction; Western creditors (particularly the private institutions) are reducing their exposure to the region; commercial banks are extremely reluctant to extend new finance to the heavily indebted Eastern European countries if there is even a slight possibility of official debt forgiveness in the future (as in the case of Poland in 1991 when the official Paris Club creditors agreed to debt forgiveness of the unguaranteed portion of bank loans for export finance); the Eastern European countries are still seeking debt-relief measures (Poland, Bulgaria), borrowing from international financial organizations and official credit agencies (particularly for Russia, Ukraine, Bulgaria and Poland) and debt reschedulings for the latter countries. Clearly, well-defined strategies as to how to deal with the present external debt situation in Eastern Europe are a necessity for both creditors and debtors.

An interesting question has arisen relating to the assessment of the region's creditworthiness. Will economic liberalization in Central and Eastern Europe lead to an abatement of pressure on the external balance of these countries in the short and medium term?

The performance of the Eastern European economies must be judged by long-term economic growth prospects rather than by gross and net debt levels. In other words, it must be judged on the efficiency of the macro- and microeconomic organization, or the system, which determines the principal questions in economic life, "What," "How" and "For whom." Eastern Europe cannot solve its transfer problem with the Western nations without making a long and difficult adjustment in economic development strategy which will increase efficiency and create a competitive production base. However, experiences in the 1970s and 1980s in Eastern Europe, as well as in many developing countries, show that the road to economic inefficiency is paved with good intentions (e.g., Poland, Hungary, Latin America, Africa).

Detailed answers to the above questions are not possible in the present study, but the following brief answers can be suggested. The economic reforms are presently in "embryonic" form. In all the Eastern European countries, the reform programs lack an entirely logical structure, clear conceptual vision and action for the future. Although reformers are intent in their endless search to help the government achieve economic progress, no magic formulas will come to the rescue of the Eastern European governments. Moreover, it will take time, as well as stability and continuity of policy, to create the foundations of new states, to adopt new constitutions and for the governments to establish the legal framework of the economy, to determine macroeconomic stabilization policy, to allocate resources to improve economic efficiency and to establish programs that will affect the distribution of income. Reactions and rejections by the parliaments of Poland and Ukraine in March 1992; the opposition in Russia to the "big bang" program (of the Gaidar government); and the opposition in the Parliament of Slovakia to a similar economic strategy in 1992 and early 1993, all point to one of the major problems for government actions in Eastern Europe: its lack of both stability and continuity of policies.

All of these countries have weak governments, and their major dilemma revolves around the question of how to achieve a consensus that, on the one hand, will provide strong, stable and consistent government, able to carry out monetary and institutional policies, and, on the other hand, will be flexible and responsive enough to absorb popular discontent through legitimate channels, avoiding dangerous extraparliamentary and antidemocratic events. In other words, the economic reforms will not change the de facto logic of the economic system and remove all centrally planned controls (which can now be called state orders) and regulations in Eastern Europe. Nor can they effectively solve the problems of bureaucratic opposition, lack of financial discipline and lack of a real market price system in the medium term.[9]

It should be stressed, however, that the main problem to be solved in this decade is not the tension in the external balance and the capital gap, but the *institutional gap* with the Western market economies and societies. With regard to the state regulations in the economy, we should not forget that removing old constraints usually leads to new ones. For example, even in the advanced Western economies, deregulation policies are considered to be politically and economically difficult to implement at present. The same applies to the developing world. The Argentinian finance minister, for example, stated in his public lecture at Harvard University in March 1993 that the introduction of his so-called Cavallo economic program in 1992, which called for radical deregulations and rapid privatization, required strong government efforts to obtain the Parliament's approval. Therefore, we should not be overly optimistic about effecting the "divorce" between the state and the economy in postcommunist Europe.

Another problem is *creating a policy elite and managerial groups* in Eastern Europe, which have adjusted to the new economic order inasmuch as the reform process requires not only a collection of radical new laws (*dekreti*) and good rules for economic management, but also people—decision makers, officials and managers—who have adjusted to these new rules. As Alexander

Hamilton emphasized, "energy in the executive is a leading character in the definition of good government."[10] The present government and managerial groups in Eastern Europe come from the old inefficient and still deep-rooted communist structures. For more than four decades, the Eastern European countries have spoken a different economic language than the knowledge-based Western (European) nations. And it takes time to learn it, and to eliminate old "dialects" and "accents."

From the economic perspective, then, we would be too optimistic to expect a radical transformation in the domestic economies and to establish the self-regulated natural order of the market, thereby improving macroeconomic efficiency in the individual Eastern European countries and in the former Soviet Union in the short and medium term. One of Eastern Europe's major problems in the first half of the 1990s will be the *creation of perfectly competitive markets* that have the remarkable efficiency properties of the invisible hand. Competitive prices reflect social costs and scarcities, and perfectly competitive markets lead to allocative efficiency.

Connected with this problem is the destruction of monopolistic structures and influences since these can drive up prices (even in a situation of restrictive monetary policy) and restrict production below the most efficient level. These policies must be carried out in a situation of a large external debt ("tax on GNP" to be paid abroad) and accumulating domestic debt, with its large capital-displacement effects. While creating a market is crucial, ownership and competition are, so to speak, secundus unter pares. As Hayek observes, "the system of private property is the most important guarantee of freedom, not only for those who own property, but scarcely less for those who do not" (1946, p. 54). In other words, since the foundations of private property, markets and competition in Eastern Europe are still in their embryonic form, serious constraints will be imposed on the efficiency of their domestic economies.

One of the most serious macroeconomic problems faced by the reforming Eastern European economies is *inflation*. The Russian economist G. Yavlinsky stated in a public lecture at Harvard in May 1993 that inflation is "enemy number one" for his country. The same can be said for the whole region. Given the serious macroeconomic imbalances in Eastern Europe, the respective governments have been tempted to increase the quantity of money, so that they can increase spending without having to rely on the highly inefficient tax-collecting system. As Milton Friedman has stated, "inflation is a printing press phenomenon" (1980, p. 254). Eliminating inflation (which is too ambitious a goal given the economic collapse in Eastern Europe), or at least reducing it to reasonable and manageable levels, is of primary significance for the success of a government's macroeconomic policies. Here it might be useful to remember the words of John Stuart Mill:

There cannot, in short, be intrinsically a more insignificant thing, in the economy of society, than money; except in the character of a contrivance for sparing time and labour. It is a machine for doing quickly and commodiously, what would be done, though less quickly and commodiously without it: and like many other kinds of machinery, it only exerts a distinct and independent influence of its own when it gets out of order (cited in Friedman, 1980, p. 249).

Soon after World War II, Ludwig Erhard's monetary reform in Germany ended open and repressed inflation. People resorted, for example, to barter and to the use of cigarettes as a medium of exchange for small transactions, and cognac for large ones. There is little evidence that such an action would have the expected effect and be sustained over the medium term in Eastern Europe. It is highly doubtful. The external and domestic imbalances in all the Eastern European countries are so serious that monetary reform will "mitigate" the sickness for short periods of time, but will protract the *inflationary recession*. The lack of stable currencies is probably the most serious economic problem of postcommunist Europe. The overall situation resembles a situation described by Keynes in 1919: "Lenin was certainly right. There is no subtler, no surer means of overturning the existing basis of society than to debauch the currency. The process engages all the hidden forces of economic law on the side of destruction, and does it in a manner which no one man in a million is able to diagnose" (1919 [1988], p. 236).

There is yet another danger in Eastern Europe: namely, non-consequent monetary policies (which are difficult to sustain, for example, because of social and political considerations such as elections) lead to a vicious cycle of another round of inflation and continuing problems of higher inflation and higher unemployment. In the conservative view of Milton Friedman, "the real option is only whether we have higher unemployment as a result of higher inflation or as a temporary side effect of curing inflation" (1980, p. 282). However, as many scholars agree, the Philips curve was not "born" in Eastern Europe; that is, higher unemployment is not accompanied by reduced inflation in these countries.

The other alternative for Eastern Europe would be to "live" with the inflation over longer periods of time, placing greater focus on structural reforms—institutional reforms, demonopolization and privatization—in the economy. This would obviously be a risky approach, carrying a high possibility of failure and provoking constraints from the international financial organizations, which would certainly insist on budget balancing and macroeconomic stability in their program. Some years ago, a finance minister in Brazil observed most perceptively: "if inflation is a horse I know how to ride it." It seems to me that Eastern Europe will be trying to tackle a similar problem in the short and medium term. The social and political tensions in the region will surely lead to a retreat from the big bang approach of the 1990–92 period.

THE NEW ECONOMIC ORDER

The question as to where the Eastern European economies will go from here can be answered in three words: to the market. That is, these economies will not be either Marxist or Soviet communist, but will to great extent resemble, in embryonic form, the Western

European economies. They will have democratic governments, an expanded welfare state, nationalized industries and government intervention of the economy.

Eastern Europe now faces many problems, which for both their people and policymakers appear to be intractable. It might be interesting to mention here the statement John Stuart Mill made more than a century ago, that "he would be a communist if he believed that economic misery and deprivation were inherent in a capitalist economy" (cited in Okun, 1975, p. 118). At least some of the Eastern European countries will ultimately discover better ways of drawing the boundary lines between efficiency and security, and between the domain of right and the domain of money. As Okun states, "It will never solve the problem, for the conflict between equality and economic efficiency is inescapable. In that sense capitalism and democracy are really a most improbable mixture. Maybe that is why they need each other—to put some rationality into equality and some humanity into efficiency" (Okun, 1975, p. 120).

As mentioned earlier, whether or not the emerging new economies of Eastern Europe can be called socialist is only a matter of taste and terminology. Past memories in Eastern Europe associated with the so-called real socialism suggest that government programs will consciously avoid the terminology.

It seems appropriate to conclude this chapter with the words of Hayek:

The economic freedom which is the prerequisite of any other freedom cannot be the freedom from economic care which the socialists promise us and which can be obtained only by relieving the individual at the same time of the necessity and the power of choice: it must be the freedom of economic activity which, with the right of choice, inevitably also carries the risk and the responsibility of that right (1946, p. 53).

In that sense, if the newly emerging democratic states in postcommunist Europe want to make radical changes in their economies and societies, the previous equalitarian principles (of the societies of "equal poverty") should be abolished. It is a difficult task as Vaclav Klaus states: "to dismantle the 'implicit' socialism in us—the habits, prejudices, and traditions built over the past decades in our political, social and economic system. . . . We need neither third ways nor market socialism dreams" (1992, p. 73). Hayek says that the term

"socialism" is often used to describe merely the ideals of social justice, greater equality and security . . . and in this sense it means the abolition of private enterprise, of private ownership of the means of production, and the creation of a system of a "planned" economy. . . . Socialism, fascism and communism all differ from individualism and in short they are totalitarian in the true sense of this new word which we have adopted to describe the unexpected, but nevertheless inseparable manifestations of all forms of collectivism (1946, pp. 25, 34).

The ongoing economic transformation in Eastern Europe seeks to establish private enterprise, private ownership, rules of law, markets, and the abolition of the "planned economy." The adjective "socialist" will obviously not be appropriate for describing the new emerging economic order.

3

Economic Reform
and Political Change

SOCIAL AND POLITICAL DILEMMAS

The economic fate of Eastern Europe and the former Soviet Union in the early 1990s, and obviously during the whole decade, will depend not only on economic and social factors but also on an equation that has too many political uncertainties to yield a clear answer. The postcommunist countries are facing the challenge of establishing democratic rule in civil societies whose political culture for many decades was determined by an oppressive dictatorship. The transformation in postcommunist Europe requires a new political language and a new political vision. The radical economic changes are taking place in a political environment that resulted from the so-called tender revolutions or velvet revolutions (as in former Czechoslovakia) of 1989 in Central and Eastern Europe and the so-called completed bourgeois revolution in the former Soviet Union after the coup attempt in August 1991. The old bureaucratic communist structures at the low and medium levels are still in place, and their stubborn sabotage of change should not be underestimated. Today there is an urgent need not only of radical institutional changes, which will establish private property and the rule of law, but also for people who as decision makers, politicians and managers have adjusted to these new rules and will give substance to the emerging new institutions.

The Eastern European countries face many political and economic problems in their efforts to establish new postcommunist societies:

• Re-establishing the rule of law

• Finding new leaders to replace old officials

• Reforming old institutions and establishing new ones

• Dealing with the remnants of the Communist party's power and the legacy of the communist period on popular values and expectations

• Finding a way to channel popular desire for change into coherent political directions and policy orientations

• Reshaping national policies in order to satisfy the national aspirations of individual national groups and dealing with the social, environmental and other problems that accumulated after more than forty years of communist rule

Social instability, ethnic tensions, hyperinflation and high unemployment rates characterize the environment in which the economic reforms with their unpredictable political consequences for the newborn democracies in Eastern Europe are to be carried out. At the international level, the recession in the Western industrialized world, the trade protectionism in these countries (Zloch-Christy, 1991, p. 93) and the increased protectionist barriers in the European Community (after the Maastricht Treaty) and in the United States (with the new Clinton administration), as well as the danger that the GATT negotiations will break down, together with the war in the former Yugoslavia, have created additional external pressures on postcommunist Europe. These are the basic dilemmas and questions that are at present confronting all of the Eastern European countries. A Hungarian scholar has summarized the economic, political and social tensions in Eastern Europe with the brief question: "Are they, in return for true freedom, prepared to give up bread lines for unemployment lines?"[1]

It is widely recognized that new democracies and new economic power and economic orders cannot be established quickly, simply because the basic preconditions for creating and sustaining democratic governments are lacking—namely, economic development, a large middle class, traditions of autonomous, pluralistic group activity and experience in limited self-government. As the Hungarian political journalist Gyorgy Konrad points out, "Our countries and societies do not have deep rooted democratic traditions. They lack democratic reflexes, philosophies and attitudes. There is no independent, developed bourgeoisie. The intelligentsia was to a great extent a 'client' of the state. The political bureaucracy still gives the tone. All that cannot be changed overnight" (*Spiegel*, February, 1992, p. 160). More than that, from the economic perspective, the economy cannot be changed overnight, for it evolves over time. At present, Eastern Europe's political liberalization is relatively more advanced than its economic liberalization and reform. But again I must stress that democracies and democratic traditions cannot be created and sustained soon in postcommunist Europe. The democratic elections of parliaments in the region after 1989 are only the first steps in the difficult process of changes. Obviously, democracy cannot be associated only with democratic elected parliaments.

NOTIONS OF WESTERN SOCIETY AND ECONOMY

Not only the radical economic changes but also the political democracies are in their embryonic form. But let me first briefly define "Western" society and economy, since the term *Western* is so often used in analyzing the transformation in postcommunist Europe. Again let me apply Hayek's definition as a theoretical foundation. In his political economy study, Hayek wrote that "Western" is "Liberalism and Democracy, Capitalism and Individualism, Free Trade and any form of Internationalism or love of peace" (1946, p. 20). In our analysis we should keep in mind that the transition to a Western European society and economy based on the three pillars of constitutional democracy, markets and welfare state is neither automatic nor irreversible. As Fischer-Galati points out, "in a period of economic uncertainty, of getting even with previous oppressors, of social readjustment, and of general nervousness and insecurity, national and international reconciliation and political stability in general are not likely to be recorded soon."[2]

COMPATIBILITY OF ECONOMIC AND POLITICAL ORDER

In examining the economic and political changes in post-communist Europe, we should consider the question of the compatibility of the economic and political order. In the classical literature on comparative economic systems, many arguments are made with respect to the correspondence or contradictions between economics, politics, law, morals and technology. Social scientists support some general ideas on the compatibility of economic and political order. In his study *The Capitalist Revolution* Berger discusses consensus on the following four propositions:[3]

1. Capitalism is a necessary but insufficient condition of democracy under modern conditions (the Weber/Friedman connection).

2. If a capitalist economy is subject to increasing degrees of state control, a point will be reached at which democratic governance becomes impossible (the Hayek connection, qualified by Schumpeter as to the quality of political leaders, the limited scope of policymaking, a well-trained bureaucracy of good standing and tradition and self-control by the members of the populace).

3. If capitalist development is successful in generating economic growth from which a sizable proportion of the population benefits, pressures toward democracy are likely to appear (the Lipset/Dahl connection). This proposition also implies that if capitalist developments are

unsuccessful in generating economic growth and a large part of the population suffers decline in living standards, pressures toward retreat from democratic traditions and toward authoritarian rule might appear.
4. If a socialist economy is opened up to increasing degrees of market forces, a point will be reached at which democratic governance becomes a possibility.

Jon Elster, who expands on the general ideas about the inter-relations between the economic and political order, suggests four notions.[4] His first proposition is that the introduction of a true liberal democracy is a necessary condition for the introduction of true markets. This implies an inverted Friedman connection: that is, political democracy is a necessary condition for legality and competitive capitalism. A complete elimination of the Communist party system is essential to economic recovery. The second proposition is Kornai's argument on the impossibility of super-constructivism, for example, the planned selection of the best elements of all existing economic orders. This proposition is reminiscent of de Tocqueville's warnings against "halfway-house solutions," such as capitalism without individual rights. The third proposition is that a mixed state of liberalism, pluralism, commer-cialism, parliamentarism and legal constitutionalism is essentially a byproduct of the existence of market and democracy. The fourth proposition is a chain-argument (von Mises-Buchanan-Weber-Rawls), and it implies that price and ownership reforms presuppose each other (in order to institutionalize the drive to rational prices and efficient allocation), whether or not we have democratic order.

Political economists and social scientists do not fully agree on the interdependence between economic and political order. On this matter, let me again turn to Hayek, Friedman and Schumpeter. Both Friedrich von Hayek and Milton Friedman have argued that democracy and free markets are mutually dependent and inextri-cably connected. Schumpeter, a member of the Austrian school of economists, has suggested that the relationship between markets and democracy may well be competitive and conflicting. He

believed that free market processes tend to generate large dispari-
ties between winners and losers, whereas democratic processes
tend to take from the winners and redistribute their gains, in the
process undermining incentives and substituting central controls
and regulations for free markets. S. M. Lipset went further and
suggested that there was no direct relationship between democracy
and markets; the one, he said, could occur without the other.

The normative approach of the present study is based more on
the Hayek–Friedman vision for the interrelation between democracy and free markets.

THE POLITICAL SYSTEM

The transformation in postcommunist Europe also brings up the
issue of the new political system and development. It is obviously
too early to present a clear answer to the questions involved in this
issue, for the Western-style elements in these new societies and
states are in their embryonic stage. Here my interest is in the
analytical framework of the political system in the newly emerging
democracies and market economies in Eastern Europe.

My approach is based on Samuel P. Huntington's definition[5] of
a political system as a system that consists of mostly institutional
elements, all of which are subject to change. He suggests five major
systemic components: culture, structure, groups, leadership and
policies. He also believes that the political development process is
strongly influenced by the interplay between these five components, and mostly by their type and rate of change.

One systemic issue that is very important for our assessment of
the political changes in Eastern Europe is the process marked by
the creation of a new political culture and the dying off of the
Moscow-dominated communist elite and mass culture—which is
obviously a contradictory and long process. Based on the Huntington definition, political culture embraces "the values, attitudes,
orientations, myths, and beliefs relevant to politics and dominant
in society."[6] Political culture also includes mass perceptions as

well as political ideologies. In this connection, a distinction should be made between elite and mass political culture.

The discussion of the new political systems and developments in postcommunist Europe also requires a consideration of the importance of the notion and necessity of new civil societies and new civic culture, which are generally recognized as a necessary condition for democracy.

CIVIL SOCIETY IN POSTCOMMUNIST EUROPE

One of the most important aspects of postcommunist Europe's transformation into a Western-style society and economy, as defined above, is the establishment of a *civil society* (given the very modest record of some of these countries such as Poland, Czech land and Bulgaria in the prewar period). Civil society will be one of the major influences on economic and political developments in Eastern Europe in the years to come. It has its domain in the public sphere and creates the basis for movement and institutional politics. The interactions between economic changes and political developments in Eastern Europe cannot be understood without considering the issue of civil society and social capital. As scholars and politicians in both East and West recognize, the transition to democratic societies depends on prior societal traditions and the emergence of a new political culture. The crucial test for consolidating and institutionalizing democracy and markets is the (relative) success of the new democratic state in the task of handling the basic economic, political, social, ethnic and diplomatic problems of the countries and making the countries governable. This is a challenge for both state and civil society, and the way the challenge is met will have important repercussions on the relations between them.

Civil society in a sense is an opposite concept of the state. As the English political scientist T. G. Ash writes, the creation of civil societies means the establishment of societies that are "Western, liberal, democratic, with a market economy based on property rights, a freely elected parliament, and an independent judiciary."[7] Social and political networks organized horizontally, not vertically (hierarchically), value solidarity, civic participation and integrity, and create the foundations for the democracy to work. Social capital as a public "good," in the sense of social organization such as networks, norms and trust (which tend to be self-reinforcing and cumulative), facilitates coordination and cooperation for the mutual benefits of the society, thus giving an answer to the prisoners' dilemma problem where everyone would be better off if everyone could cooperate, and enhances the benefits of investment in physical and human capital. Thus, it can be regarded as a vital ingredient in a country's economic development. Developing the embryonic forms of social capital in postcommunist Europe cannot be regarded as a substitute for effective public policy. Rather, it is a prerequisite for it, and to a point it is a consequence of it. Moreover, creating social capital should begin at the grass-roots level, and not within the government. The postcommunist societies should make a strong effort to build social capital and not leave the respective countries to the mercy of historical forces.

Since the issue of new civil society in Eastern Europe is so important, I would like to make some conceptual additions to the above definition. Civil society was first used as a synonym of political society, and later its meaning shifted to that opposite to the concept of the state. As mentioned above, it is this latter meaning that tends to be in current use. Victor Perez-Diaz suggests two forms of civil society.[8] In the first form, civil society denotes a set of the following sociopolitical institutions: first, a limited government or state operating under the rule of law; second, a set of social institutions such as markets (or spontaneous extended orders) and associations, based on voluntary agreements among autonomous agents; and third, a public sphere in which these agents debate among themselves, and with the state, about matters of public interest, and in which they engage in public activities.

This definition is employed by the actual sociopolitical systems of Great Britain and the United States, and as scholars widely accept today, corresponds to the essentials of the blend of liberal democracy and market economy which is typical of contemporary Western societies. The term *civil society* implies that the society includes autonomous agents—citizens—as opposed to subjects of despotic rulers and so on. These citizens are autonomous agents, and they may act in an autonomous manner vis-à-vis the state, because the state has only limited power to enter these agents' reserved domain.

In the second form of civil society, its markets, associations, and a sphere of public debate are less developed and exist within the framework of other historical configurations, such as those presided over by authoritarian and totalitarian regimes (for example, Franco's Spain and the pre-1989 Eastern European societies).

One might argue that this second form is emerging in Eastern Europe and that it is a necessary transitory form that is preparing the way to a liberal democracy and a full-fledged market economy, and the establishment of the first form of civil society.

Voltaire once stated that "man is free if he needs to obey no person but solely the laws." The newly emerging democracies in Eastern Europe have to travel a long road to achieve such a freedom in a civil society.

ASSESSING THE EFFECTS OF ECONOMIC TRANSFORMATION AND POLITICAL RISK

The problem of evaluating political risk and assessing the effects of economic transformation were first discussed in detail in Zloch-Christy (1988, Chapter 6 and 1991, Chapter 4). Additions to these chapters are as follows.

With regard to the *assessment of the effects of the economic reforms*, we should carefully analyze not only changes at the macro- and microeconomic levels, but also any changes in the foundations of the Eastern European states. We should examine their institutional gap with the West and the performance of the governments in Eastern Europe in order to determine whether there are radical market-oriented changes in exercising their four basic executive functions related to the economy:

- To establish the legal framework of the economy
- To determine macroeconomic stabilization policy
- To affect the allocation of resources to improve economic efficiency
- To establish programs that affect the distribution of income

In assessing the political risk, it is essential that we examine the country's leadership and political developments in postcommunist Europe. Associated with the problem of evaluating the country's leadership (as discussed in Zloch-Christy, 1991, Chapter 4) are several interesting questions relating to the assessment of political developments in the individual Eastern European countries: Are the changes in the economic and political system revolutionary, or can these developments be called political decay? Is there any potential conflict between the power elite and the country's elite? How can the new states form coalitions with different social groups? Are there any rebellious movements against the government, and why do people rebel? Is there any crisis of legitimacy for the government and the new country elite? (This is a serious question for almost all of these countries with deeply rooted communist structures.) Does dual power exist, or do new political powers emerge (e.g., executive president Yeltsin and legislative president Khasbulatov)? Is the political system dominated by the Parliament or by the president (e.g., Uzbekistan's presidential rule, where the government and the regional governments, the so-called khokimiyat, are appointed by the president)? What is the role of the trade unions in the economy and politics, and are they still dominated by the nomenklatura? Can loss of faith in the government's policy be observed, and are there any internal "riots" among the ruling elite? Are there any developments indicating a breakdown of the state (e.g., former Czechoslovakia in 1991–92)? What is the position, influence and political will of the former secret police (e.g., KGB) in the country? What is the state and political will of the army (e.g., the former Soviet army after the breakdown of the union)? What is the state of the former communist structures in the economy and in the society, particularly in the government, Parliament, army and secret police? Are there any tendencies toward creating regional blocs in postcommunist Europe (e.g., Central Europe, the Baltics, the Asian republics, Russia and some of the former republics)? Are the social changes in the country characterized, for example, by the replacement of the older communist ruling class by a new ruling class—in other words, does a de facto social revolution take place (since there cannot be Eastern European capitalism without Eastern European capitalists)? How advanced is the process of creating civil society and social capital? How quickly will the old institutions be destroyed and replaced by new institutions, values and political elite?

Let me briefly discuss a few of these questions in evaluating political and economic issues in postcommunist Europe—the emergence of new regions, the role of the former secret police and the role of the army. The emergence of new regional developments should be carefully monitored, since regionalism seems to be the basis for economic development not only in postcommunist Europe but also in the world in the not so distant future.

Embryonic forms of regional economic and political developments are in evidence in Central Europe and in the former Soviet Union. The Central European countries Poland, the former Czechoslovakia and Hungary signed the so-called Trilateral Cooperation Agreement in February 1990. In August 1990 the Pentagonale agreement was signed by Austria, the former Czechoslovakia, Hungary, Italy and former Yugoslavia; Poland joined in 1991, Ukraine in 1992, and Bulgaria, Romania and Germany's Bavaria asked to participate in various projects. In 1992 the Pentagonale was renamed the Central European Initiative (CEI). In February 1993 a new agreement involving broader cooperation was signed by the Ukraine, the Slovak republic, the Czech republic, Poland and Hungary. The CEI remains, however, the broader cooperative agreement in the region, focusing on the following areas: transport and telecommunications, the environment, small and medium-size enterprises, scientific and technical research, culture and tourism, information, energy, and migration.

The Central and Eastern European countries also signed an agreement of cooperation with EFTA and an associated agreement with the EC. The Baltic republics of the former Soviet Union have developed intensive contacts with the Scandinavian countries and Finland, which represents another possibility for regional cooperation. In June 1992 some of the Southeastern European countries—Moldova, Ukraine, Bulgaria, Georgia, Greece, Albania, Russia and Romania—as well as some Asian countries—Turkey, Azerbaijan and Armenia—established the Black Sea Economic Cooperation Scheme, with a focus on the environment, transportation, communications, energy, information science and technology, agriculture, tourism, and health. It also sought to set up free trade zones, with free movement of labor, goods, capital and services, and to create the Black Sea Trade and Investment Bank for promoting trade and capital transactions. A new economic cooperation agreement involving the former Muslim Soviet republics—Azerbaijan, Tadjikistan, Turkmenistan, and so on, is yet another possibility in the region. Russia's role and influence (e.g., for Tadjikistan, Kazakhstan) or Turkey's role (e.g., for Uzbekistan, Turkmenistan) should be carefully analyzed in that respect. If the Russian republics were to split up, a number of new smaller states and regions would be formed in, for example, Chechenya (which declared full independence in March 1993), Tataria, Karelia, Bashkiria or provinces like Nizhny Novgorod (which have their own economic reform visions) (*New York Times*, 15 March 1993, p. A6). Regional developments will be extremely important for the economic and political stability of postcommunist Europe and the former Soviet Union.

Let me now turn briefly to the role of the secret police and the army in the country. Undoubtedly, political developments in Eastern Europe will be profoundly influenced by the decommunization of these institutions, although as yet we have no evidence that their decommunization is very advanced. The former KGB with its more than 500,000-man "army" of servants still has the power to impose its political will on the Russian government, and on the former Soviet republics which established new security institutions after the breakdown of the Soviet Union and, respectively, the republics' KGB. It has been speculated, for example, that not long after the August 1991 coup attempt, some KGB colonels organized themselves in an underground organization, which has de facto control of this institution. The deeply rooted communist structures within the secret police and the army were also not destroyed in Bulgaria, Romania, the former Czechoslovakia, Hungary and Poland. Thus, dangerous grounds for political opposition to liberal and democratic government policies have been laid. The disintegration of the Warsaw Pact and of the former Soviet army, and the plans to reduce, for example, the Russian army to only 1 percent of the population (or 2 million people), as well as Russian troops abroad, are generally positive steps. However, the social discontent among the former Soviet officers (who are easily exposed to populist slogans) should not be underestimated and should be carefully monitored for future developments. The same is true of the other Eastern European countries.

Conflicts between the former Soviet republics as regards, for example, the Soviet nuclear weapons arsenal (e.g., Russia and the Ukraine have disputed the ownership of the two thousand strategic nuclear weapons on its territory), Russia's exports of nuclear and modern conventional arms or the "brain drain" to some Third World countries are important issues that have political consequences not only in the region, but for the world as a whole. Plans for a collective security system in the former Soviet Union or in the other regions in Eastern Europe (if any) should also be carefully monitored.

Another country-specific question that needs to be examined is that of ethnonationalism and of possible *ethnic* or *religious* disturbances in the individual Eastern European countries. In several of these countries (e.g., Russia, the Ukraine, Armenia, Romania, Hungary, the Czech republic, the Slovak republic and Bulgaria), ethnonationalism has emerged as a major force to engage people in politics. Particularly strong are the nationalist movements in Slovakia, Russia, the Ukraine, Hungary and the Baltics. Political leaders in these countries are making use of the nationalist card in their policies. For example, Moscow alone publishes thirty-eight fascist newspapers that are devoted to manipulating Russian nationalist feelings. Surprisingly strong nationalist groups are those in Hungary which have made anti-Semitic and other attacks against minorities. Almost all of these countries face potential unrest owing to disturbances caused by ethnic or religious conflicts and by the poor state of the economy and declining production, exports and small influx of foreign investments. According to some estimates, for example, foreign investment in the amount of U.S.$7 billion in the period 1990–92 was directed mainly to Central Europe (with Hungary getting 60 percent of it) rather than to the former Soviet Union—Russia, the Ukraine, the Baltics, the Asian republics and so on (*Financial Times*, 10 March 1993, p. 3). The power vacuum that emerged after the breakdown of the former Soviet Union has provided the grounds for new ethnonationalist movements, particularly in the former Soviet Asian republics and in Southeastern Europe. All these developments indicate that a new approach to our analysis of the economic reforms, political developments and country risks in postcommunist Europe is essential.

THE ECONOMIC COSTS OF TRANSFORMATION

As most scholars agree, the transformation in Eastern Europe is faltering. Economic progress is lacking in the former Soviet Union, at best is only modest in Poland, Hungary, Bulgaria and the former Czechoslovakia, and is only at the beginning stage in Romania (despite the fact that Romania was the first Eastern European country to outlaw its Communist party, on 12 January 1990).

Why? It is obvious, as was stated earlier in this chapter, that the economy evolves through time. And in order to determine whether the transformation is slow or rapid, we should compare the Eastern European economies with other transforming economies. Obviously, it is also a philosophical issue. Since there is no other precedent in history of changing a command into a market economy, it is difficult to make comparisons. From an economist's point of view, the changes since 1989 can be considered to be relatively slow. But why is the progress so slow? Were economists too optimistic in late 1989? To approach this question let me first discuss briefly the issue of the economic costs of transformation, after which I will suggest an answer dealing with the issues of "What can be done" and "What should be done" in terms of economic policy.

The bad record of Eastern Europe's economies since 1989 and in the former Soviet economy, particularly since 1991, can be explained through five simple factors, some of which are not likely to be transitory:

1. Investment. The rate of aggregate domestic investments has fallen and is negative in all the countries. In the late 1980s, the Eastern European economies had certain capital stock, and a new demand structure has emerged. Since the capital stock structure is durable, however, time is needed for it to adjust to the new demand structure. Compared with some developed and developing economies, the rates of aggregate domestic investments, for example, in the Southeast Asian newly industrialized countries, Japan and the United States, were on average 30 percent, 24 percent, and 16 percent, respectively.

2. Savings. The savings rates have fallen and are negative in all these countries. (Domestic savings in GNP in the late 1980s, for example, averaged 30, 28, and 13–14 percent, respectively, in East Asia, Japan and the United States.) Thus, the basic rules of economic stability involving work, investment and savings have apparently been "forgotten" in Eastern Europe. To save and produce seems to be the only strategy to combat the deflationary pressures.

3. Labor. Eastern Europe's workforce, though trained, literate and industrious, is undisciplined, which represents a serious problem. The political scientist Alex Pravda describes the working population of Eastern Europe as thoroughly spoiled. He argues that the special kind of "social contract" operative there by which the population is paid little but also does not unduly exert itself has put the workers in such a rut that it is difficult to move them to more effort.[9] From an economist's perspective, this statement cannot be fully accepted, since new market macro- and microeconomic policies affect actors' behavior in the economy. But, of course, it will take time to move the workers, civil servants and intelligentsia in Eastern Europe to more effort.

Unemployment reached more than 9 percent in 1991 and in 1992–93 was expected to increase to 14 or 15 percent. Poor worker morale, lack of individual responsibility in the workplace and the deep-seated egalitarianism fostered by the former communist system are serious obstacles in the efforts to reform the economy and improve economic performance and efficiency.

4. Management. Eastern European managers are energetic and competent, but they lack experience in domestic and international competition, and they have not yet adjusted to the new market rules. Under the centrally planned economic system, monopolistic structures and sellers' markets, they did not, of course, learn to raise product quality and cut production costs.

Building knowledge and know-how in the postcommunist economies will be slow, and there is a need for an exchange of information among agents. Decisive steps are also needed to encourage entrepreneurship in small industries.

5. Nationality conflicts, particularly in the Commonwealth of Independent States, the former Czechoslovakia, Hungary and Romania.

Other factors which impose obvious constraints on the Eastern European economies are the accumulated external debt and the breakup of the former Council for Mutual Economic Assistance's (CMEA) system for multilateral trade and payments (in the so-called transferable rubles), which have exacerbated the crisis for the individual countries. Exports and imports from the former

CMEA countries were sharply reduced by some 30 to 40 percent in 1990–92. Eastern European economists and policymakers recognize the importance of adjusting to the "CMEA shock" (which at a conservative estimate caused a 3 to 5 percent decline in GNP; this percentage, of course, varies in the individual countries). Because of the economic and political instability of the region, however, few pragmatic and rational steps, such as regional cooperation agreements, were undertaken in this regard. In May 1992 Czech economist and politician Vladamir Dlouhy observed that "the former Soviet market remained crucial to Czecho-Slovaks economic development, even while the country was trying to shift its attention to more attractive Western markets." Politicians of the smaller Eastern European countries and the former Soviet republics echoed this thought.[10] The collapse of the interregional trade in the case of the former Soviet Union may cause a decline in national income within these new countries of some 30 to 40 percent. Russia, though less affected than all the other countries, has still experienced a falloff in its trade with these countries, which will hurt its already troubled economy. Again, only Russia, Kazakhstan and Ukraine will apparently experience some gain in trade with relative trade prices, with the other republics shifting to world prices.

The sharp decline in trade among the Eastern European countries and the former Soviet republics may be compared to the situation that occurred in Central Europe after the breakdown of the Austro-Hungarian empire in 1918. In that period, the nationalist tensions in the region had real implications for the economies of these countries. Tariffs, quotas, exchange control and transport barriers were the tools used to break established trade relations and to develop autarchical domestic economies. Economic analysts of the mid-1920s described the situation as follows:

Post-war commercial policy . . . has largely been based upon the idea of economic self-sufficiency, and has sought to make the new national units independent not merely in the political but also the economic sphere. The attempt to carry out this policy naturally produced chaotic results in an area such as Austria-Hungary, which had hitherto enjoyed complete freedom of trade.[11]

This historical analogy clearly reflects the present economic and political danger for postcommunist Eastern Europe and the former Soviet republics. The chaotic results are everywhere evident, but the lessons of the breakdown of Austria-Hungary are obviously lost on the Eastern European leadership.

ECONOMIC POLICY: WHAT CAN BE DONE AND WHAT SHOULD BE DONE?

One of the most important objectives in postcommunist Europe is to establish a program as well as an alternative to that program for the reform. I do not suggest that there should be a "new plan" for change (the "planning economies"). Obviously it is difficult in a rapidly changing domestic and international environment to make plans. The reform program of the individual Eastern European countries, considering their individual conditions, should encompass necessary macroeconomic changes in both the short and medium term. These programs should serve as their "compass" on the new road they have now embarked on; without such a "compass" the new economic and political leaders in Eastern Europe will easily lose sight of their vision for the future, given the enormous economic, political and social factors they must consider on a day-to-day basis. The result could be "zig-zag" policies.

Creating and defending such programs is obviously politically difficult. Even one of the most radical reformers in Eastern Europe, Vaclav Klaus, states that such programs are not needed:

We do not believe in sophisticated sequencing of economic or reform measures. We know that just as an economy cannot be centrally planned so an economic transition cannot be centrally planned and administered. The economic transition is a process with many forces, many constraints, many policies. We have to react, and react rationally. There is no computerized program saying that at the beginning, one must introduce measure one or measure two, three, four, or five. I prefer to compare reform, traumatic radical reform, with chess. One simply has to know how to play (1992, p. 75).

Although this is an interesting statement, we must not forget that to play chess well-established rules must be followed. And the reason for the programs is to establish rational and programmic rules for change (e.g., industrial policy, privatization and foreign investments) in postcommunist European economies.

Thus, programs for economic transformation should clearly define strategies for dealing with the five factors discussed above and create the necessary macroeconomic environment for making changes in investment, savings, labor and management—all of which is easier said than done. The economic reforms in all the Eastern European countries and the former Soviet Union do not have a well-defined model nor is an alternative model readily available. This is probably too difficult a task for the Eastern European politicians, especially in view of the poverty of the political scene in these countries. Because of the system under which they lived for so many years, there are few politicians of true value in postcommunist Europe.

It is assumed that the transitional costs of transforming the command economies will be both high and protracted. Yet, in a recent study, the American economist Charles Wolf (1991) demonstrated that, when properly measured, these costs (in the accurate sense of opportunity costs) should be much less than many Eastern European and Western scholars and officials have estimated. Wolf may well be correct. In their favor, the postcommunist countries have traditional links with Western Europe and potential for economic recovery. Moreover, the favorable state of the East-West political dialogue provides the necessary stability for the economic transformation. The main issue is that the process of transformation should be pursued along the lines of a sophisticated program for monetary, fiscal, price, and wage policies, as well as for privatization, a new social security system, and exchange rates and currency convertibility policies.

Most scholars agree that the successful transformation of the postcommunist economies depends on simultaneously adopting six policy instruments: (1) monetary reform (control of the money supply and credit); (2) fiscal reform, tax reform to encourage entrepreneurship, policies to ensure budgetary balance and to limit monetization of the government debt); (3) price and wage liberalization to account for costs and to boost productivity; (4) privatization and policies to eliminate monopolistic structures and to open domestic enterprises (state and private) for foreign competition; (5) social security policies (particularly for the unemployed); and (6) exchange rate unification and convertibility on the current account to link the domestic economy to the world market. Creating new institutions and establishing new constitutions and laws are crucial to the success of this six-policy package.

The coherent implementation of sound monetary and fiscal policies is also important, as are institutional changes, privatization, an efficient banking system, new infrastructure (including environmental protection) and a climate of freedom that will enable the actors in the economy to pursue their personal goals. Creating an environment of competition for the domestic agents (state and private) and exposing them to foreign competition should be two other important goals.

Ronald McKinnon (1991) makes a lucid case for sound monetary and fiscal policies preceding all other changes in the depressed economies of Eastern Europe and the former Soviet Union. McKinnon also demonstrates the relevant experiences of Japan, of other Asian countries such as Taiwan and of some Latin American countries (Chile). The lessons of these various experiences to the Eastern European countries is that productive capacity cannot resume until the depreciation of money and the resulting economic demoralization come to an end. Establishing property rights is another important early task of economic transformation. As Hayek wrote, private property and Western-style democracy mutually depend on each other: "the system of private property is the most important guarantee of freedom . . ." (1946, p. 54), and ". . . neither good intentions nor efficiency of organization can preserve decency in a system in which personal freedom and individual responsibility are destroyed" (p. 92).

There is a need to protect property rights and to establish the rule of law and the rule of contracts in Eastern Europe. As one of the first American lawyers stated more than two hundred years ago, without private property there will be no justice. There is an urgent need to establish an objective market measure for government policies. The main problems, however, are to create not only markets but also a secure system of private property. As was stated earlier, the market is crucial, but ownership is *secundus inter pares*.

One of the main objectives of the new government programs in the short and medium term should be to elucidate the necessary steps that will combine macroeconomic stabilization, radical economic reform changes and policies that will promote the move from stabilization to growth. In this regard, the following questions should be addressed:

What steps will ensure stabilization and radical change in the macroeconomic system? What should their sequence be?

What are the key policy measures needed to restore growth?

What is the contribution of the external environment (e.g., international financial institutions), and what role can debt relief and stabilization loans play in supporting a program?

It is important to select the most appropriate stabilization package, in the framework of the overall strategy for industrial policy (if any), privatization and other radical reform changes. Dornbusch contends that the design of a stabilization effort should comprise five elements:

- The poststabilization inflation target
- The extent and manner of fiscal stabilization

- The appropriate monetary policy
- The appropriate level of the exchange rate
- The use of an incomes policy[12]

The design of such a reform and stabilization package is extremely difficult but not impossible. As most economists believe, there is no quick route from stabilization to growth, and the transition remains difficult to understand and even more difficult to accomplish. Again, let me turn to Dornbusch, who states:

Countries that have experienced protracted high inflation, financial instability, and payment crises will not find their way back to growth easily. Their economies need to achieve not only fiscal reconstruction by thorough budget balancing but also a far-reaching institutional reconstruction that involves a financial system able to provide efficient intermediation and a regulatory and trade regime that helps allocate resources to maximize productivity. When external resources are in short supply, making the most of the country's resources through *better allocation of resources* is the only way of raising the standard of living. Fortunately, in the aftermath of mismanagement, the scope for such productivity enhancement is often substantial.[13]

These remarks fully apply to the postcommunist European economies.

In the optimistic scenario, economic "reconstruction" will take at least a decade. The stabilization, restructuring and growth of Eastern Europe will also depend largely on external debt relief measures and stabilization loans (e.g., from the IBRD and EBRD). Although sustainable economic growth and development should be primarily self-financed and be generated endogenously, in a situation of large disequilibrium in the external balance short-term financing obviously cannot be avoided.

In this connection, it might be interesting to return to the historical experience of the Austro-Hungarian empire. In 1919, when Joseph Schumpeter was serving as a finance minister in the First Austrian republic (Die Erste Republik), he wrote:

Without external assets there can't be a stabilization of currency and hence no order in the public finances. The reverse sequence, first to establish internal order and then to seek external credit is a path of desperate dissipation which has been taken all too often in financial history. The fateful vicious circle, no external credit, no internal order, but without internal order no external credit must be solved. The State must find external credit whatever severe the burdens that must be imposed on the citizens (cited in Seidl and Stolper, 1985, p. 346).

Study of Central Europe's economic history after the First World War also suggests that in postcommunist Europe at present external financing should be directed to reducing budget deficits and external balance deficits. Other measures should involve establishing low tariffs and quotas, fixing the exchange rate, avoiding overvaluation, balancing budgets, creating an independent Central Bank (also discussed in Chapter 5) and imposing some exchange controls. All these measures will bring positive results for the economy and political situation and help solve social problems, in both the short and medium term.

With regard to privatization, scholars and politicians are debating how to attain this important goal but quite unanimously agree that without privatization the former communist economies will remain inefficient, producing poor quality goods and enduring a lot of poverty. In all the Eastern European countries, privatization of small firms (mostly in trade and services) is already under way, as is the so-called spontaneous privatization. Ian Winiecki observed that the state enterprises, in an effort to stave off bankruptcy, have begun simply to sell their assets to private companies and in effect have been privatized (*The Economist*, 23 January 1993, p. 15). The restitution laws have either restored property to their former owners from the 1940s and 1950s (Bulgaria, the former Czechoslovakia, Poland, Romania, Russia) or have awarded financial compensation (as in Hungary). The privatization of small-scale enterprises in Russia (dominated, as in the other countries, by the "red nomenklatura" and insiders) is also making progress. Data on privatization in Russia, as well as Hungary and Poland, are presented in Tables A.4–A.8.

Thus, the first steps in the emergence of a new middle class in Eastern Europe which will provide support for the democratic governments have already been taken. However, the private sector remains relatively weak and is not playing a political role; its special interests are not reflected and represented in the parliaments of these countries. Nonetheless, the main issue is that the Eastern European countries do not have a clear program for privatizing the large enterprises. They do not, for example, have an industrial policy. The question that therefore arises is, can and should large enterprises be rapidly privatized?

Before trying to answer this extremely difficult question, let me briefly mention the Czech and Russian programs for privatization proposed in 1992. The Czech program envisages that 8.5 million people will participate in the transfer of $10 billion worth of state assets to private shareholders. The Polish scheme is similar to the Czechs' in principle. Romania announced voucher privatization in early 1993. Similarly, in August 1992 the Russian president stated that "tickets to a free economy" in the form of vouchers would purchase 10,000 rubles each beginning on October 1, 1992 (*The Financial Times*, 21 August 1992, p. 12).[14] The voucher system has a number of drawbacks, however.

- It cannot help spread wealth among the people.
- It cannot inject new skills into the economy.
- It cannot create tradeable financial assets.

Voucher programs are rather speculative schemes, and, as is true of lotteries, do not usually generate wealth in the economy. A Russian and Czech retreat from such privatization schemes might not be a surprise in the not so distant future.

The problem of commercialization versus privatization cannot be answered in a clearcut way. Here the most important consideration centers on how much the economic efficiency will be increased by rapid privatization or market policies and by exposing state enterprises to domestic and international competition. The experiences of China and other countries in Southeast Asia, as will be discussed in the next chapter, are relevant in this regard. I will share the view of those who in the case of strategy for rapid privatization of large industrial enterprises remember the old wise words that "haste makes waste." In a modern society, the role of the government should not be considered an "externality" in the reform package. Government policies are urgently needed to keep the economy going during the reform stage. Such policies will enable not only destructive but also constructive moves during the transition.

The approach to the privatization of the large state enterprises should be one of gradualism. An important aspect of such a strategy is that the large Stalinist "giants" should be first restructured and then privatized. The governments in postcommunist Europe should be preoccupied not so much with the monetary aspects of the reform package (and to "walk on one leg") but with balancing the budget, tax reform and tax administration (to increase revenues), and growth in productivity. The real issue is to make shifts on a sectoral level without triggering a deeper depression. Growth will come from the private sector, and in this regard incentive financing is important. Even in some developed Western European countries (e.g., Italy, France, Austria and Scandinavia) during the last forty years a large overstaffed, relatively inefficient state sector has been balanced by a dynamic, innovative private sector. China's experience in the 1980s and the early 1990s is also interesting here.

Government should preserve social order, impose contracts and enable the financial system to "work." In addition, in Eastern Europe the state, while pursuing a policy for gradual privatization of the large state enterprises, should have strong policies that will help keep the state enterprises and bureaucracy from destroying the state from the inside. One plausible strategy would be to increase the autonomy on the local level—regions, provinces, municipalities—and to remove the center's responsibility while the economy is in a deep depression or while the state structures are collapsing (as in the former Soviet Union).

Anticorruption government policies are also essential. Corruption in the emerging market economies has become a "twin" of democracy. As the experience of many developed and particularly of developing countries shows, corruption may prove to be not only socially erroneous but also costly to development. The high corruption in Russia and Eastern Europe, for example, can hamper investment and economic growth there. The illegality of corruption and the need for secrecy have made it very distorted and costly in the former communist economies, whose governments are very weak.

Imposing financial discipline in the postcommunist economies is yet another serious issue. The state and private enterprises should be aware of the government's commitment, if they are negative value added and inefficient, and financial support (bailouts) should be provided by law. New laws on banking, accounting and bankruptcy are needed. In particular, there is a need to establish an apparatus for the enforcement of bankruptcy procedures.

In summary, government policy in Eastern Europe should focus on

- Setting new rules, regulations, and incentives
- Providing technological infrastructure
- Creating a climate for competition and local rivalry, stimulating (aggressive) investment and innovation
- Formulating industrial policy and challenging industries (see Chapter 4)
- Attaining decentralization and local autonomy

Accordingly, governments should play an important role in the early stages of the transformation process. Government influence in the economy is clearly in evidence in many countries of the world—not just in postwar Japan, France, Southeast Asia and New Zealand, but also in the United States. As Samuelson states ". . . many commentators wonder whether the excesses of the recent era have propelled America into a new radical age in which Congress will legislate against businesses and which governments will over-turn market forces" (1989, p. 483). The liberal Harvard economist John Kenneth Galbraith goes even further, stating that today's economy is directed by large bureaucracies, not by perfectly competitive markets; technostructure guides countries of both East and West (cited in Samuelson, 1989, p. 829). At the end of the twentieth century with its numerous economic, social, political and environment problems, the libertarian ideas of the nineteenth century could not have deep roots in the economic and political life of the Western countries, postcommunist Europe, and the developing world. As the Swedish economist Assar Lindbeck notes, there is some mistrust of both the market and state bureau-cracy, but these two systems are the only mechanisms known to society that allow a complex modern economy to allocate its resources (cited in Samuelson, 1989, p. 832).

Eastern Europe also has an urgent need for sophisticated civil servants to replace its many incompetent bureaucrats and commu-nist officials. Of particular importance is the need to replace middle and upper level bureaucrats, levels that at present are totally occupied by former communists. In other words, there is a need for "new wine" in "new bottles." Here we should mention the experience of France and Japan, where civil servants enjoy social prestige and come from the elite schools. It might not be so difficult to achieve such a goal soon in the postcommunist Europe. Communism created structures but did not give them content and did not set roots in the society. The new economic environment and the democratization processes have changed the situation in a fundamental way. However, it will take time to create a new civil service system; here cultural and historical factors will play a role in the individual countries.

As for the costs of the economic transformation, they remain high because all of the Eastern European countries are conducting their reform programs without the synergy that would be provided by the six major policies discussed earlier. Moreover, there is a lack of clear vision in the areas of stabilization, industrial policy, privatization and productivity growth. As Wolf states, such a reform implementation is "like trying to swim with only one arm and leg" (1991, p. 6). Monetary policies made without structural and institutional changes may combat inflation (temporarily), but they also lead to increased unemployment and sharp decreases in production and consumption. In other words, they do not eliminate deflationary pressures. They remain only as successful anti-inflationary programs, but not as comprehensive programs for economic transformation. The IMF policy changes made in June 1992 with regard to Russia suggest that both East and West recognize these shortcomings (*The Financial Times*, 23 June 1992, p. 6).

All the reforms lack both a clear concept and an alternative concept for privatization and foreign capital inflows. The issue of privatizing the industries is one of the most important in this regard. No doubt there is a need for pragmatic policies and for partial government regulation and intervention in particular areas and in particular cases. And no doubt, too, the reforms require time. Not all inefficient (slightly negative value-added) enterprises should be scuttled; rather, they should have a chance to improve their performance.

Among other things, leasing should be considered as an alternative for privatization and as a transitory solution for both medium- and large-scale enterprises. Leasing in its various forms would give the industries a chance to "survive" in the new economic environment. An especially pragmatic option is that of buying equity after the leasing period expires. This approach would motivate the investors to look toward potential ownership and would therefore increase their interest in investing. As is well known, leasing is a financial arrangement widely used in the West.[15] In the case of Eastern Europe, leasing could substitute for the lack of private domestic capital and the relatively weak foreign investment flows into the region. It could also serve as a transitional alternative for the rapid privatization plans of some of these countries, especially the former Czechoslovakia. As a Bulgarian economist pointed out in an informal discussion in 1992, "to privatize in our countries means to sell something whose owner is unknown, and whose price is uncertain, to people who have no money." Leasing could help solve this dilemma.

Leasing could also enable civil society (and government indirectly) to deal with the "red nomenklatura" which now dominates the trade unions throughout the region (a partial exception being at some point Poland). At the same time, the government could deal with the issue of replacing the "red nomenklatura" managers on the medium and upper levels, training new managers, and creating a new managerial elite. All such action may produce a "solidarity pact" among government, employers and trade unions and thereby put reform and financing on a sound footing. In addition, through leasing for example, in a five-year period, some political goals for a gradualistic approach to privatization could be achieved. For example, the "red nomenklatura" could be prohibited from acquiring state assets. Through the schemes mentioned above for privatization in the Czech republic, Russia, Poland, and Romania this cannot be avoided. (In Poland, even though the Parliament did not approve the privatization of six hundred large state enterprises in early 1993, it is still not clear whether the concept for voucher privatization has also been abandoned and other approaches will be discussed; see the *New York Times*, 19 March 1993.) Leasing, for example, can enable the reformers in postcommunist Europe to avoid making the industrial complex a serious opponent of the economic changes and source of potential political tensions.

State industry plays an important role in the national economies of Western Europe. In 1992 a French industry minister predicted that "if the 1980s were dominated by financial questions, the 1990s will be the time for states to intervene in industry in the same way as they do in finance, as regulators—but not just as regulators, as co-ordinators as well" (*The Financial Times*, 8 June 1992, p. 28). Eastern European economists and policymakers would do well to study the French experience and the French notion of the state as shareholder. Such an approach would be especially appropriate for the smaller Eastern European countries, considering their history, state of development and European culture.

Harvard professor Lawrence Summers, former high official of the World Bank, also supports government intervention: "We have lost sight of the role of government's supporting hand in our enthusiasm for the 'invisible hand'; some government intervention is good and that is as true in the United States, as it is in Mali" (*Business Week*, May 1992, p. 78). And it is obviously true in Eastern Europe as well.

One pragmatic solution to the "survival" of the inefficient state industries in Eastern Europe, for example, would be to introduce government regulations for bonuses for workers in state firms, based on cost-profit considerations.[16] At the same time, through legislation and fiscal and monetary policy, the government could actively support the emergence of new private enterprises. The new private sector will naturally and gradually absorb the workers from the inefficient state sector. At some point, this will solve the problem of mass unemployment in Eastern Europe. The present monetary policy (e.g., high interest rates) in most of the Eastern European countries does not facilitate private business activities. In this regard, some corrections in the framework of the stabilization–reform packages are required.

Remembering the views of von Mises and Schumpeter from the Austrian school of economics that there is a necessity of private ownership for static and dynamic efficiency, it is important in the Eastern European context to create factor markets alongside product markets. Markets in capital and land are essential to obtain the correct values of fixed assets ("von Mises' revenge"). The lack of factor markets removes Schumpeter's engine of development, his "gale of creative destruction."

"WHAT IS GOOD FOR THE COUNTRY"

Every Eastern European country must conduct its program for economic transformation according to its specific conditions and guided by the (Konfutian) principle "what is good for the country." Europe's nations have a tradition of a pragmatic attitude to life going back to Aristotle's Greece, the country that invented democracy. In this regard, it is surprising to read the statement of the Polish president Lech Walesa in *Le Mond* of September 1991, in which he blamed the Western nations for bad advice in conducting economic reforms and privatization. The individual Eastern European countries are hampered by many economic and political constraints as they try to answer the questions "What can be done?" and "What should be done?" However, only they can get the credit for any success and only they can be blamed for any failure or even for accepting advice, be it good or bad for their countries. Only the individual countries can solve problems of accumulating domestic savings and increasing investment and of creating new political cultures. Only they can answer the question of legitimacy of power, and only they can solve the problem of lack of decent administration and profit-oriented banking networks. Without decent administration even the best legislation cannot be implemented properly. The lack of a profit-oriented banking system leads to a serious political issue: indirectly financially supporting the ex-communist network that has the best connections to the banks. In other words, the present economic situation in the postcommunist countries is not so much underdeveloped but *mis*developed, and in some of the countries, as in Poland and Russia, there are many examples that can best be described as ungovernable.

The region also has too many political parties; they are very fragmented, and it is difficult for them to reach consensus. For example, in the elections of the fall of 1991 in Bulgaria, more than forty political parties were registered; more than fifty in Poland and Hungary; and over sixty in the former Czechoslovakia. In contrast, in Western Europe, the United States and Japan, only two or three major parties dominate the political scene.

All that indicates that we economists were not too optimistic in late 1989 because we considered only what makes good economic sense. But there is now a practical problem that affects the individual Eastern European countries and relates more to the politics than to the economics of transformation. Former communists or those connected to the former communist elite may at present call themselves "socialist" or "opposition," but they are among those who will be the losers in terms of power, privilege and prestige, if the reforms are properly conducted. As Wolf states, "While they may use the rhetoric of markets and competition, their interests induce, if not compel them to temporize, to delay, and perhaps to incapacitate the transformation process" (1991, p. 8).

In a recent interview, a Bulgarian politician emphasized: "How can we make reforms on a microeconomic level when 95 percent of the firms' directors are still the old communists?" This same picture applies to all the Eastern European countries. The percentage in some of them (e.g., Hungary) may be a little lower, but the statement that "the old communists are the new capitalists" applies to all of them. In the former Soviet Union lurks the danger of a new dictatorship under the slogan of "democracy and markets." As public opinion polls in Russia showed in mid-1992, some 58 percent of the respondents stated that they would support a new coup (*The Economist*, 11 July 1992, p. 49). Russia's strong industrial complex, secret police, army, and former communists dominate the Russian Parliament and so the political will for change is lacking. The same is true of the other Eastern European countries as well. This is not surprising, for the process of destroying the old communist world, including the state structures, laws and attitudes is relatively slow. In the case of Russia, the danger is that the liberal intelligentsia, the driving force behind the political, economic and social changes, is turning chauvinist.

Populism is spreading throughout the Eastern European countries, although its influence varies from country to country. The new populist leaders and organizations, though professing to speak for the people, also represent a form of authoritarianism, a situation that may lead to a form of "totalitarian democracy." In countries like Romania, Slovakia and Hungary, populist traditions are well rooted in the prewar political culture. In the case of Russia, as many historians have noted, autocracy can be viewed as a key to understanding Russian identity. This makes it difficult to develop a new political and civil culture, with all the consequences for the new democracies and civil societies. In these countries the population may well grow tired of the experiment in democracy and turn to new forms of authoritarian or one-man rule. As recent elections in these countries show, voter turnout is low (about 40 to 48 percent, for example, in Hungary), and the communist or the renamed communist parties or political groups, using populist slogans, are trying to regain power in the Parliament and government (as in the Baltic states, Bulgaria, Slovakia, Romania, Russia and the Ukraine). Such tendencies may be avoided if the economic reforms succeed and there is at least hope that living standards will be improved in the short and medium term. Otherwise, it will be extremely difficult for the Eastern European governments to control the "syndrome of mass politicization" in their countries, which leads first to social frustration and then to political instability, if no channels for meaningful participation open up. As Kornai writes, "Inflation, shortage, and stagnation or decline of the standard of living increase public discontent. The economic tensions generate political tensions; they can lead to an explosive outbreak of strikes and demonstrations. Ultimately, the economic crisis can spark off a political crisis" (1992, p. 569).

When we consider the economic strategy (and mainly the so-called "shock therapy") in its political dimension, we see that the present deflation in postcommunist Europe will trigger unavoidable political and social unrest. In the present shock therapy scenario the issue of inflation is very important, especially the hyperinflation in Russia. However, the issue of growth should also be regarded as important. After the stabilization stage, governments should focus on generating growth. As economists usually agree, there is no evidence for the proposition that disinflation can be accomplished without incurring a dramatic loss in economic growth. Pragmatic macroeconomic policies, of course, should not tolerate any level of inflation. But pragmatism tells us that growth matters and that it matters very much.

Postcommunist Europe, after the stabilization stage, should also consider the option of accepting some moderate inflation and of focusing on productivity growth, competitiveness, and increased inflow of foreign investments. As the experiences of some developing countries show, bold macroeconomic changes stressing the financial aspects of reform lead unavoidably to a classical deflationary story and hold the danger of a new crisis. Future economic historians will therefore have to agree whether the strategy of shock therapy or of gradualism would have been better for the individual countries, most of whom, particularly the Southeast and the Central European countries after the First World War, have experienced all possible crises: crisis in industry and banking, inflation and unemployment. Later they regarded this period of deflation policy as a mistake. The answer to the question of whether the present Eastern European economic strategy is a mistake belongs to the future. I would guess, however, that the analysis of future economic historians will not differ considerably from that of their colleagues in the interwar period. For the present, Eastern European governments should pursue two immediate goals: (1) to encourage the private sector and gain its support and (2) to weaken bureaucratic structures, which as was discussed early, retain power and are becoming very corrupt. Enlarging the private sector in the economy and increasing the autonomy granted to public and state firms will create a self-generating process for reducing the power of the old communist bureaucratic structures.

ALTERNATIVE POLITICAL DEVELOPMENTS

What are the alternatives for Eastern Europe and the former Soviet Union during the 1990s? There are actually no alternative ways for them other than the way of economic and political transformation. Many scholars do not share this view.[17] Despite the difficulties described in Chapters 1 and 2, and in the present chapter, I would like to argue that domestic and international conditions will force the Eastern European countries to implement the liberalization changes. As mentioned earlier in this chapter, we do not necessarily have direct proof for the relation between economic efficiency, prosperity and democracy, if we look at the map of the world today. For example, India and Israel have socialist rather than market economies, but they have democratic political structures; South Korea, Taiwan, Chile, Singapore and South China have, or have had for protracted periods, authoritarian, nondemocratic governments, but market-oriented economies. Even so, there is no doubt that political freedom and economic freedom are closely related. In this regard, the support of the Western nations for the newly emerging democracies is essential in our increasingly interdependent world.

In the case of the European postcommunist countries, any failure of democracy will cause a failure in economic transformation, and vice versa. Aid measures and debt-relief measures, among others, are urgently needed there. Some interesting proposals have been made by the chief economist of the Export-Import Bank of the United States as regards opening up Western markets for the products of the Eastern European countries and facilitating the provision of Western export credits to the region.[18] In the years to come, Eastern Europe's trade policies with the Western countries will remain the Achilles' heel of the adjustment policies of the region.

Politicians and economists stress the importance of coordinated Western policy toward Eastern Europe. In 1992–93, former president of the United States Richard Nixon several times urged the United States to help Russia solve its problems. In an article in the *New York Times* (5 March 1993, p. A29), he wrote that the Western countries "must wake up" because Russia is the key to global stability; therefore, he recommended that aid to Russia not be postponed. Aid to a free market economy in Russia could be seen as an "investment in prosperity for the United States," he said. As Nixon explained so compellingly:

Forty-five years ago, the U.S. adopted the Marshall Plan to insure the survival of freedom in Western Europe. By doing so, we gained allies in the cold war and trading partners who fueled our post-war prosperity with purchases of American products. Those same interests, peace and progress, are at stake today. If President Yeltsin's reforms succeed, we will save tens of billions of dollars in defense spending and create hundreds of thousands of new jobs to supply Russia with the new capital and consumer goods it will require. If the reforms fail, a new despotism will take power in Russia, threatening its neighbors, sending our peace dividend down the tube and providing aid and comfort to totalitarian rulers in China and elsewhere (*New York Times*, 12 June 1992, p. A25).

Similarly, former British prime minister Margaret Thatcher suggested that aid to Russia be seriously considered (*Times*, 8 March 1993). All that indicates that pragmatic solutions to deal with the financial aspects of Western support to the Russian and the other postcommunist European countries' economic and political transformation are urgently needed.

As history always tends to do, it repeats itself. The Great Powers faced similar problems after the First World War. John Maynard Keynes wrote in 1919 that "the blockade of Russia, lately proclaimed by the Allies, is . . . a foolish and short-sighted proceeding; we are blockading not so much Russia as ourselves" (1988 [1919], p. 293). Then the dilemma was how to deal with communist Russia; today the dilemma is how to promote and encourage democracy in postcommunist Russia and Europe.

The Economic Report of the U.S. President in 1982 made the following statement regarding the relationship between economic liberalization and democratization, which should be applied in our approach to developments in postcommunist Europe:

Any comparison among contemporary nations or examination of the historical record demonstrates two important relationships between the nature of the political system and the nature of the economic system: 1. All nations which have broad-based representative government and civil liberties have most of their economic activity organized by the market. 2. Economic conditions in market economies are generally superior to those in nations . . . in which the government has the dominant economic role (cited in Samuelson, 1989, p. 829).

4

Economic
Development Strategies

Will political development materially affect the rate of economic growth in the region? What are the possible economic development scenarios in Eastern Europe in the first half of the 1990s?

ECONOMIC GROWTH PROSPECTS

Many people are deeply concerned about political developments in Eastern Europe and the former Soviet Union. Political development is, of course, important in its own right, since as Evsey Domar stresses, "economic change without political change is impossible" (1989, p. 13). However, it is unlikely to have much effect on the rate of economic growth and economic development strategies in the 1990s. The major factors that will affect economic growth in the region are:

- Human resources (labor supply, education, discipline, motivation)

- Natural resources (land, minerals, fuels, climate)

- Capital formation (machines, factories, roads)

- Technology (science, engineering, management, entrepreneurship)

It goes beyond the scope of this study to elaborate in detail how these factors relate to the economic growth prospects in the region and in the individual Eastern European countries. I will also not discuss developmental paradigms such as Keynesian development strategies, neoliberal, neoclassical, or monetarist approaches to long-term developments, and their relevance, for example, for the development of Third World countries after the Second World War and particularly in the 1980s. Mainstream economics has become unable to deal with the fundamental issues of sustainable economic growth and is concerned exclusively with short-term flows of income and expenditures and their balance in various markets. No single economic theory can be considered as one that could be universally applied in our analysis of economic growth development strategies in postcommunist Europe. The proposition for universality seems not only to be controversial but also to obscure our understanding and analysis of economics in this part of the world. This is true both for the post-Keynesian import-substitution economic philosophy and for the recent neoliberalism. While post-Keynesianism at least considers the fundamental structural characteristics of the economies in individual countries, neoliberalism seems to ignore their common and particular characteristics.

The two important factors of capital formation and technology, given the old stock and technology in Eastern Europe and the expected restricted ability to borrow abroad, are responsible for the very low expectations for economic progress in the 1990s. Capital formation will be a limiting productive factor, especially in view of the region's sparse natural resources, although the former Soviet Union is an exception in this respect. The region's greatest promise lies in its human resources: the workforce is both well educated and skillful. Here we can fully agree with Domar when he states that "a country's most important factor of production is not its physical capital but its human one—the able, educated and trained manpower—and that its economic performance depends heavily on the use made of it" (1989, p. XV).

All the same, solving the human problem in Eastern Europe, in the sense of using the skills and training of its population, will take time. Acquiring a middle-class mentality with all that implies—ambition, willingness to accept discipline, ability to work hard and efficiently, to learn, to save and invest—will be a long process. In the optimistic scenario, some positive effects on economic growth can be expected in a decade. Economically useful employment of knowledge requires capital, and skillful labor is in principle much more productive when it is combined with more capital. The reduced opportunity to borrow abroad because of the large external debts, and the shortfall in domestic savings associated with low investment rates and low mobility of the factors of production mean less investment in the 1990s. Servicing the external debt requires not only the achievement of a substantial trade surplus, but also the transfer of a substantial part of domestic savings abroad (the tax on GNP to be paid abroad).

The present stabilization and adjustment programs in post-communist Europe, with the partial exception of Russia, involve dependent, underdeveloped countries. They are carrying out these programs at a time of deep recession in the industrialized world, and constrained private and international capital markets, which show at some point little understanding or willingness to contribute to investments in the region. On the other hand, there is no evidence that domestic savings can be generated. The marginal savings rate has to increase substantially in the troubled postcommunist economies in order to maintain a high level of investment (as well as to service external debts), and to be able to achieve an average domestic savings rate that exceeds the average investment rate. Therefore, high capital accumulation in Eastern Europe, which is a central issue for growth and economic development, seems to be an unrealistic goal for this decade.

Obviously, the deep recession in Eastern Europe and the region's deflationary adjustment policies have reduced personal incomes, business profit, tax revenues, and, consequently, savings. The social and political costs and instability associated with such policies are obvious. This kind of development that benefits only a small minority in the individual countries while bringing serious hardship to the majority of the population might prove not only economically but also politically difficult to be sustained over the medium term. The process of permanently changing Eastern European governments is also on the political agenda in the region, and so nonconsequent government policies can be expected.

The above observation justifies the conclusion that less investment means less growth and less wealth in the Eastern European region. In the optimistic scenario, Eastern Europe will be able to overcome the recession by the mid-1990s and to close the welfare gap that emerged after the new economic reforms were introduced.

The rate of economic growth in Eastern Europe depends largely on the nature of both the existing and the new economic institutions that allow market-oriented profit-seeking activities to take place. These economic institutions, solidified by urban interests in particular, as well as by the rural residents, are unlikely to be seriously affected by foreseeable political changes. Bureaucrats from the "old guard" will be continuing to try to incapacitate the transformation process. At the same time, some of them and the emerging group of new civil servants will be among the first to benefit from this process inasmuch as they belong to the best educated and best connected groups in Eastern European societies. The central political authorities, which also represent the new democratically elected parliaments, will not likely move the economic system backward to the old-style Soviet central planning.

These countries, and especially the former Soviet Union, face the danger of new coup attempts, but it is unlikely that this threat will thwart the effort to develop a functioning market economy. The road to a market economy will be long, but Eastern Europe will not stray from it. As Gorbachev stated after the failed coup attempt in August 1991, the leaders of the coup failed to take into consideration one very important factor: that life in the Soviet Union has changed, and its people have changed. The relatively rapid elimination of the old monopolistic structures and their state subsidization, together with replacing old bureaucrats with new people, increasing autonomy, and first of all, establishing a new political culture, will be important factors in stabilizing the economic reform process. In the early stages of this process, however, all these changes will not significantly affect the rate of economic growth.

DEVELOPMENT STRATEGIES

What are the prospects for economic development strategies in Eastern Europe? As noted earlier, applying the universality of economic theories to the analysis of economic growth and development is highly problematical. However, some of these theories, for example, Rostow's takeoff theory, Gerschenkron's relative backwardness theory and Kuznets's balanced growth theory provide some solid ground for considering this important question. Again, however, since they are not comprehensive theories that can give universal explanations for the history and future of the individual countries, each postcommunist European country at present should be viewed individually with its own special resources and needs, requiring policies that fit the particular country's unique background, culture, economic resources and political changes.

Guided by Ockham's Razor, let me consider the pattern of economic development in the postwar period, and let me ask whether such an economic development could be possible for Eastern Europe as well. Accordingly, I will describe the major economic development features in five countries or group of countries and compare them to those in Eastern Europe. The countries are[1]

- Southeast Asian NICs
- Portugal and Spain
- Chile

- Latin America (other than Chile)
- China

The main characteristic of economic development in Southeast Asian countries is their outward orientation. Portugal and Spain improved their economic performance in the 1980s after becoming members of the European Community (and democratizing their societies). Chile conducted successful policies for economic stabilization and growth after 1973; for a long time during their implementation, the country was ruled by the political dictatorship of the Pinocet regime. In the last twenty years, Latin America (other than Chile) has experienced a continuing decline in economic growth, unemployment problems, high inflation, external debt problems and increasing poverty, with oligarchy dominating the societies. Democracy is weak in this part of the world, and military coups and government corruption are rampant. Finally, China is pursuing a policy designed to gradually transform its central planning economic system and establish the foundations of a market economy in the early 1990s.

The Southeast Asian countries are the great success stories of the postwar world economy. According to Samuelson, only a generation ago East Asia's per capita incomes were one-fourth to one-third that of the wealthiest Latin American countries. Large saving rates and outward strategies enabled them to overtake every Latin American country by the late 1980s (*Financial Times*, 15 June 1992, p. 6).

Will the Eastern European countries be able to transform their economies and to pursue an economic development strategy like that of the East Asian countries? The East Asians have mixed economies, par excellence, and rely on markets to innovate, imitate, produce and sell their products, while the government provides fiscal and monetary guidance and steers the economy in the desired directions. In the case of Eastern Europe, the most important factor for economic growth is a promising one: human resources. In contrast, the other three factors—natural resources (land, minerals, fuels, climate), capital formation (machines, factories, roads) and technology (science, engineering management, entrepreneurship) — are a cause for some pessimism. In advanced market economies, economic growth is determined largely by the growth of inputs, particularly labor and capital, and by technological change.

Another interesting question that arises centers on whether Eastern Europe can achieve and sustain savings in capital formation totaling 20 to 30 percent of GNP (the rate of the East Asian countries).[2] The answer at least for the present decade is obviously no.

Yet another question is whether the region will be able to take the following growth-encouraging steps: (12) increase net national investment and the savings rate by one-third of GNP; (2) increase civilian research and development by one-fifth; (3) lower unemployment by 1 percent; (4) eliminate all strikes; and (5) reduce military spending and increase government investment. The answer is probably no. Military spending will probably be reduced, particularly in the smaller Eastern European countries and probably in the former Soviet Union and Russia as well, as indicated in the June 1992 Bush-Yeltsin meeting and following agreements. But all the other factors will be difficult to achieve in the 1990s. Social tensions will make strikes unavoidable. For example, the Austrian "social partnership model" (*soziale Partnerschaft*) for peaceful negotiation among representatives at the national level of the workers' trade unions (*Arbeitnehmer*), of the owners (*Arbeitgeber*) and of the state will only be a model, with little pragmatic application in real life. Lack of capital will make it difficult to increase government investment and civilian research and to reduce the unemployment rate.

What can the Eastern European countries learn from the successful *non*market approaches of the Asian economies, especially Japan, Korea, Taiwan, and Singapore? This region apparently has found the delicate boundary where government attempts to interfere with the market mechanism will solve problems. In the centrally planned economies, government intervention causes more problems than it solves. S. Katz, an expert on the Southeast Asian economies, stresses that "although many cultural, political and social differences separate Eastern Europe from East-Asia . . . in terms of how to go about transforming a backward economy into an efficient, competitive one, there is much common ground and many lessons to be shared" (1991, p. 5). He also states that the Asian NICs have demonstrated that market-driven economic restructuring can be achieved without incurring unacceptably high economic and social costs. This problem is, of course, perhaps the major economic, social and political problem in Eastern Europe at present. The postcommunist European countries would greatly benefit from the experience of the Asian economies by pursuing the following national priorities: high savings and investment rates; aggressive exporting; and relative self-sufficiency in food.

All the Eastern European nations need a clearly formulated set of industrial strategies and policies that will help their industries (e.g., protection from import competition, export incentives and tax relief) as well as state intervention to help diversify or phase out and retrain workers. Government also needs to provide transitional support to help the domestic enterprises adjust to a market environment.

The exchange rate policy should be an important tool for encouraging exports and savings and discouraging imports. The individual countries must also define their foreign investment policies. As Katz states, "neither Asia's NIC's nor Japan entrusted to the market or to foreign investors responsibility for deciding which of their industries would prosper and which would fail" (1991, p. 5). In this regard, it is useful to study Japan's and the Asian NICs' experience in acquiring foreign technology through licenses, franchises, market-sharing arrangements and the like. For example, in the late nineteenth century Japan imported European bankers as advisers to help create a domestic banking system, but not their banks.

As regards creating financial markets, it might be interesting to explore the experience of these countries in establishing stock and bond markets as intermediaries to promote business and raise capital. This issue is of particular importance for the financially underdeveloped economies of Eastern Europe, where a specialized investment opportunity might go unexploited for lack of capital. Developed stock markets, for example, are important for growth, since they create information about investment projects and therefore put investors' funds to better use, thereby raising the rate of return to economy-wide investment.

On the matter of price liberalization and subsidies, it should not be lost on Eastern Europe's policymakers that prices in Japan and the Asian NICs are influenced as much by national budgets as by market forces. Key prices are further adjusted by fiscal means (tax rebates, tariffs, duties and subsidies). This principle applies not only to the Asian economies, but also to the agricultural pricing policies of the United States and of the European Community (EC) and many other developed countries such as Austria, Switzerland and Sweden. In the case of Japan, the price of rice, and the very high prices of fruits, vegetables, and similar commodities, is influenced primarily by government intervention. Any government proposal to cut subsidies to agriculture always faces serious resistance from the Japanese peasantry with its large electoral power.

Eastern Europe and especially countries like Bulgaria, former Czechoslovakia, Hungary, Poland and Romania could greatly benefit from membership in the EC and could successfully be reintegrated into Europe during the 1990s. Former Czechoslovakia, Hungary and Poland became associate members in the first half of 1992, and negotiations were successfully completed with some of the other countries later in the year. Bulgaria and Romania's prospects for admission are also good. As for the former Soviet Union, given its size, nationality conflicts, and political tensions, it is difficult to speculate if and when it or any of its former republics will become an EC member. Some analysts believe

Russia should become a member of the G7, and others have proposed a new organization, established in the West, that would deal not only with the economic aspects of Russia's transformation (for example, the IMF) but also with its political dimensions.

Western Europe is, in principle, interested in supporting the aspirations of the smaller Eastern European countries to participate in Europe's strongest economic union. Former British Prime Minister Margaret Thatcher at an early date recommended that the European Community offer membership to the emerging democracies of Eastern Europe "clearly, openly and generously" (*The Financial Times*, 6 August 1990, p. 1).

The smaller Eastern European countries therefore have a good chance to follow the pattern of economic development set by nations like Spain and Portugal. The Eastern European politicians understand that their future economic development will depend greatly on their standing with the EC. Membership in the community will speed up their economic and political reforms and help them adjust to their new realities. However, the hope that some of the smaller countries will soon become a "second Spain" and repeat its "success story" may be overly optimistic. Eastern Europe's changes began only two or three years ago, whereas Spain and Portugal have well-established market structures and some economic stability, with priority given to productivity growth and low inflation. These countries have become attractive for rapid inflow of EC capital in the second half of the 1980s, and they took steps to restore civil society long before they joined the European Community. For example, the period 1975–85 was a time of democratic consolidation for Spain, and the Catholic Church played a stabilizing role in this regard. Moreover, in Spain the left has abandoned the idea of radical transformation and has lost its illusions about the socialist world. Spain also has a good corps of civil servants, which has created the basis for the future Spanish Eurocrats.

Undoubtedly, the smaller Eastern European countries could well follow the Iberian nations' economic path.

While association with the European Community has potential benefits, the economic relations among the former members of the Council for Mutual Economic Assistance, dissolved in early 1991, should not be broken. Accordingly, several proposals have been made to create a European Payments Union. As McKinnon states:

Not all the lessons learned from the Marshall Plan are relevant for economic assistance to Eastern Europe today. But the similarities—the need to overcome trade diversion and to establish internal macroeconomic control before liberalization can proceed—are worth studying. Some collective Marshall-type financial mechanism for restoring "normal trade" among the existing Eastern European states is the most pressing need on the political agenda (*Wall Street Journal*, 16 July 1991).

Also beneficial would be a multilateral payments union among the smaller Eastern European countries, which would follow the successful experience of Western Europe in the period 1950–58. Such a union in which, for example, some Western European countries would participate, would help overcome trade diversion and establish internal macroeconomic control before liberalization proceeds any further in Eastern Europe. The participation of the former Soviet republics could also be considered. The political feasibility of such a union is a question for another discussion. One of its political aspects centers on the EC's own problems regarding the Maastricht Treaty of 1991 which was so difficult to negotiate. Other political considerations are the troubled reunification of Germany and the acceptance of new members like Austria and Sweden in the 1990s. (For details on an Eastern European multilateral payments union, see Chapter 5.)

Many scholars regard Chile as an economic success story—and probably the only such success story in Latin America. After the fall of the communist government in 1973, Chile achieved macroeconomic stability, trade liberalization, privatization of state industries and currency stability. However, it took the country more than fifteen years to do so. Interestingly, Chile's economic progress was realized under the dictatorship of General Pinocet's military government. Chile's so-called people's capitalism proved that to make state-led privatization work it was necessary to concentrate executive power and authority and that, surprisingly, the state may become even stronger in implementing such policies. Chile's experience also demonstrates that the issues of state regulation are relevant and deserve attention. It illustrates that a direct relationship between economic prosperity and democracy is not necessarily required.

Chile's pattern of development will probably not be repeated in the Eastern European countries, particularly the smaller ones. Given the democratic European traditions after 1945 and the favorable climate for better economic and political relations between Eastern Europe and Western Europe, political dictatorships in the postcommunist countries are not likely, especially in the smaller Eastern European countries. The prognosis for the former Soviet Union in this regard is not as clear. One senior Chinese government official, in fact, stated in October 1991 that Yeltsin's rule is reminiscent of the old autocratic rulers of Tsarist Russia. While I cannot speculate here about Yeltsin's future political behavior or that of his future successors, I should point out that it would be highly useful for Eastern European politicians to carefully study the experience of Chile in its search for macroeconomic stability, and particularly its fiscal, monetary, and privatization policies.

One can only hope that Eastern Europe during the 1990s will avoid the experience of the other Latin American countries, especially Argentina with its deflationary policy, nor should the region copy some other extremes like the protectionism and import-substituting state industrialization of the 1920s, 1930s and the post-World War II period, or retain economies and societies based on deeply rooted income inequalities.

The economic situation in Latin America has steadily deteriorated in the last two decades, and prospects for sustainable stabilization are very gloomy. If the process of economic transformation and political reforms in Eastern Europe encounters serious difficulties, then economic instability, oligarchical structures and Latin-style political tensions might present themselves in some of the Eastern European countries. One might hope that countries like Hungary, the Czech republic, Poland, and Bulgaria will be successful in repeating the development patterns of Spain and Portugal, but if they fail their situation will be the same as that in Latin America. In such a situation, a large inefficient state sector and large subsidies for agriculture will be the outcome. As regards the former Soviet Union, social tensions and economic and political chaos could lead to protracted Latin American-style macroeconomic instability.

Given China's relatively successful economic development during the 1980s, could it also become a model for Eastern Europe and the former Soviet Union? In the 1980s China implemented a strategy for gradual reform of its centrally planned system. It was thought that the majority party bureaucrats and the population would block market-oriented reform if it were implemented by "big bang" style policies. The thinking was that by adopting a gradualist approach the same reform could succeed. In China, gradualism has been regarded as politically a more stable strategy. In other words, this is a macroeconomic policy made up of small but feasible steps ("What can be done?"), and at some point it has become a strategy of "no haste, no waste" and of "divide and concur" (i.e., agricultural reform, followed by reform of industries in the 1980s, and so on).

Senior Chinese politicians observe that their country is an island of tranquility in a sea of world chaos. Indeed, economic growth in China has been impressive in the recent years. For example, industrial production increased 19 percent in the first eight months of 1992 as compared to the same period of 1991, and output from heavy industry and light industry rose by 21.3 percent and 16.3 percent, respectively. In the same period, coal production, electricity and production of nonferrous metals increased, respectively, 10.8 percent, 10 percent, and 18.3 percent (*New York Times*, 10 September 1992, p. D14). These figures are impressive, especially when we consider the deep recession that began in Eastern Europe and the former Soviet Union in 1990–92.

China dismantled the rural collective system in 1978 (only twenty or so years after Mao imposed it), established a two-tier price system (determined by market forces and state regulation), did not privatize state enterprises but put enormous emphasis on facilitating autonomous local enterprises (nonstate economy) tied to the growth forces of the world market, encouraged foreign investments and greatly benefited from trade with the world's most dynamic economic area, the Asia-Pacific region. Banking reform, including the establishment of an independent Central Bank and a separate commercial bank system, is on the present agenda. While Eastern Europe could learn a great deal from China's experience, especially from the facilitation of the large nonstate economy, communist-style political dictatorships such as China's do not appear to be a probable model for Europe's post-communist countries.

5

Currency Convertibility in the Postcommunist Economies

After addressing some principal political economy issues in the previous chapters, I will discuss in this chapter[1] one of the most interesting macroeconomic issues in the present economic reforms, namely, currency convertibility.[2] I will also address the question of what the West could do to assist Eastern Europe during its transition, since currency convertibility and domestic economic reforms are strongly interrelated. The success or failure of the economic reforms will be measured by the improvements made in economy efficiency. As conventional wisdom tells us, economic efficiency will thrive where currency convertibility comes at an early date.

This chapter addresses the following questions:

- What were the Eastern European concepts for introducing currency convertibility in the pre-reform period? (Brief overview).

- What are the advantages and the preliminary macroeconomic conditions for convertibility?

- What are the possible scenarios (measures and stages) for achieving convertibility?

- What international support is needed in the transition to convertibility?

Some of the most important areas of modern macroeconomic policy are exchange rate policy, currency convertibility and multilateralism. For more than four decades, these issues were of no practical importance for Eastern European policymakers and of almost no theoretical interest for Eastern European scholars. Until the early 1960s CMEA countries were undergoing rapid structural changes and pursuing strong autarky tendencies, which made the discussion on currency convertibility less pressing. However, after the mid-1960s with slower CMEA economic growth rates, economic efficiency and trade gains (both with the CMEA and Western partners) became important issues that led to greater attention to problems of convertibility. In 1971 a major policy objective of the so-called Integration Program was to introduce currency convertibility (for both the national currencies and the CMEA "international" currency, the transferable ruble) in the CMEA region in the medium term. In practice, however, most Eastern European economists and policymakers saw the issue of convertibility as a goal for the very distant future. In the late 1970s Hungarian banker Janos Fekete stated that "convertibility in the Western sense would introduce such spontaneous elements into our planned economies which we cannot undertake" (cited in Holzman, 1978, p. 160). The first experiments designed to improve central planning in most of the Eastern European countries after 1985 (Gorbachev's reform) focused greater attention on the issue of convertibility, which became a high topic again after the Forty-third Session of the CMEA in 1987.

In implementing the Herculean task of transforming a centrally planned economy into a market economy, what strategy is needed as regards the currency convertibility? Given the favorable climate in East-West relations, what international support can be considered in the transition to convertibility?

THE CONCEPT OF CONVERTIBILITY

Multilateralism, transferability and convertibility are closely related concepts, with convertibility usually implying both multilateralism and transferability. According to the International Monetary Fund (Gold, 1971, pp. 1–2), in Article VIII, sections 2, 3 and 4, IMF members are obliged to avoid restrictions on international transactions, multiple currency practice and discriminatory currency arrangements. The monetary authorities of a member country must convert balances of their currency when those balances are presented for conversion by the monetary authority of another member. Currency convertibility requires that the following three criteria be satisfied: (1) It can be used without restrictions of a currency character for any reason whatsoever; (2) it can be exchanged for any other currency without restrictions of a currency character; and (3) it can be used or exchanged at its par value, at a rate of exchange based on the par value, or at some legal rate of exchange defined in any other way that is considered desirable.

Briefly defined, currency convertibility means that there are no restrictions on holding, using, or exchanging it for another currency. The freedom to exchange domestic currency into another currency may initially be given only to nonresident holders, but the right may then be extended to residents. In other words, the road to establishing full convertibility of the currency involves eliminating all or substantially all restrictions on the holding, using or exchanging of it for another currency.

Two main forms of convertibility are possible, as well as several combinations among them: financial (currency) and commodity convertibility. Financial convertibility refers to the freedom to convert the currency into foreign exchange, whereas commodity convertibility is related to the freedom to convert the currency into goods on the domestic market. That is, financial convertibility signifies the absence of restrictions on the exchange of one currency for another, while commodity convertibility requires lack of restrictions on the use of the currency. In market economies where the currency is already commodity convertible (in contrast to the centrally planned economies), establishing currency convertibility involves the introduction of financial convertibility. The experience of market economies shows that this financial convertibility is established first for nonresidents and is then extended to residents. In other words, a fully convertible currency is both financially and commodity convertible for both residents and nonresidents.

The Issue of Convertibility in the Pre-reform Period in Eastern Europe

This section briefly discusses the CMEA's attempts to establish convertibility before 1985 and the present policy. This overview provides the background for my approach to the question of how to make the Eastern European currencies convertible. A detailed discussion on the pre-reform period goes beyond the scope of the present study since these issues have already been extensively analyzed by economic historians, experts and scholars, in both East and West.

Since the 1960s, the Eastern European countries had tried to establish a multilateral settlement system for trade and payments. The desirability of currency convertibility was generally accepted in Eastern Europe during the 1960s, and its advantages were seen by CMEA policymakers and scholars, first, as part of the process of modifying the central planning system in order to achieve an efficient economy, and, second, as a way to use CMEA convertible currency to finance trade flows to reduce dependence on the currencies of the Western countries. However, Eastern European economists at that time were in less agreement on how currency convertibility was to be achieved, or even exactly what it was. In the early 1970s Soviet professor Yuri Konstantinov, then chairman of the CMEA Commission on Currency and Financial Problems, emphasized that specialists of CMEA countries "must formulate the very concept of currency convertibility under the conditions of a planned socialist economic system, a state monopoly of foreign trade and a foreign currency monopoly" (cited in Allen, 1974, p. 21). Soviet economists at that time made a distinction between socialist convertibility (*obratimost*) and capitalist convertibility (*konvertiruemost*) by arguing that the former, unlike the latter, is "planned" and not subject to "capitalist market anarchy." Some Eastern European countries, notably Poland in 1965 and 1968 and Hungary in 1969, made proposals to their CMEA partners aimed at increasing the financial convertibility of the transferable ruble (TR).

The 1971 CMEA Program for establishing multilateralism and currency convertibility was a failure, primarily because the CMEA countries were unable to reform their centrally planned economies, eliminate the bilateralism in their trade and payments relations or create multilateral trade areas. The modest CMEA achievements vis-à-vis multilateralism, transferability and convertibility have been related to the noncommercial CMEA exchange rates set in the mid-1970s, the currency coefficients between the Soviet ruble and the TR (modified several times during 1971–89), the CMEA joint investment currency coefficients from 1973 (and their subsequent modifications) and the 1972 agreement regarding limited financial convertibility (for tourist travel for residents and CMEA nonresidents) equivalent to 30 Soviet rubles, 27 Bulgarian leva, and so on.

The Issue of Convertibility in Light of Present Economic Reforms

Their modest experience and achievements as regards convertibility are obviously a source of serious concern for the individual Eastern European countries, given the present complexity of political and economic issues in the domestic economies, in intra-Eastern European relations and between East and West. Eastern European policymakers realize that in implementing market-oriented reforms, convertibility has wide-ranging implications for economic and political processes and is an important tool of macroeconomic policy as regards proper market signals and efficient resource allocation.

All of the Eastern European countries announced that they planned to introduce convertibility in the medium and long term. Poland was the first to implement a bold market reform, with convertibility being the most important element of its program in January 1990. Hungary has a more or less unified exchange rate, and its regulations on holding, using and exchanging the forint for another currency have been steadily liberalized. For example, the domestic commercial banks in Hungary are no longer required to submit their convertible currency reserves to the Hungarian National Bank and can now buy and sell convertible currencies freely. However, firms are still required to surrender their convertible currency revenues for forints to a commercial bank, although they can buy convertible currency freely when they need to pay for imports. The banks' exchange rates will be based on a largely free foreign exchange market (RFE/RL Research Report, Vol. 1, No. 28, 10 July 1992, p. 53).

Bulgaria and the former Czechoslovakia, after joining the Bretton Woods institutions in 1990, took steps to obtain a unified exchange rate, which as in all the other countries in postcommunist Europe was set up as a floating rate, and currency convertibility (given the requirements of Article VIII of the IMF agreement). In Romania plans for currency convertibility (and more important their implementation) are still not clear; almost no changes have been made from the pre-1989 period.

In the former Soviet Union the situation is also unclear. In Russia the Gaidar government made the introduction of ruble convertibility a high-priority policy objective in the short term. In the former republics, including the Baltic states and the Asian republics, despite agreements with the IMF, minor steps have been taken to achieve unified exchange rates and currency convertibility, the obvious reason being the difficult economic and political situation there. In Russia the more than three thousand currency coefficients were removed on 1 January 1992, and five exchange rates were introduced (plus the official exchange rate). Plans for a fixed and later a floating ruble exchange rate beginning on 1 July 1992 were postponed for an unspecified period. In July 1992, the Russian government announced that it "had given up hope that the ruble would become fully convertible in 1992 at a rate around 80 rubles to the US Dol" (RFE/RL Research Report, Vol. 1, No. 32, 14 August 1992, p. 68). A more realistic exchange rate was considered the auction level, which in July 1992 was double the figure stated above; that is, it was more than 160 rubles per U.S. dollar, and the market rate in early and in mid-1993 reached the level of some 500 and 1000 rubles per U.S. dollar, respectively. Auctions, though a step in the right direction with regard to introducing currency convertibility, also impose restrictions on holding, using and exchanging the currency, because of the rationing of currency, in other words, inconvertibility. Selected enterprises are allowed to compete for foreign exchange. In July 1992 some currency restrictions were removed in Russia, and a regulation was passed stipulating that for the purchase of amounts of up to $500 no documentation would be required for a Russian citizen. However, those traveling abroad would be forbidden to take more than $500 out of the country without special authorization (RFE/RL Research Report, Vol. 1, No. 32, 14 August 1992, p. 68). Hence, a policy to introduce currency convertibility in Eastern Europe is evident in the first stages of the economic reform process.

The predictions, however, made by the Russian economist A. Aganbegyan in the late 1980s as regards ruble convertibility are still valid today. Aganbegyan wrote that one of the most frequent questions he has been asked in many discussions both in the former Soviet Union and abroad is whether the ruble will become convertible, and if so, when (Aganbegyan, 1989, p. 209). He answered that ruble convertibility would likely be introduced in the next seven to ten years and in stages: first, "domestic" convertibility (commodity and financial convertibility), followed by convertibility with the former CMEA countries, and finally, convertibility with all other countries (Aganbegyan, 1988, p. 41). He also stressed that some were considering the creation of either a second currency, a "hard ruble" backed by a combination of gold and foreign currency reserves and by exports, or a "parallel ruble" devoted entirely to foreign trade and capital transactions— like the *chervonets* currency used during the New Economic

Policy (NEP) period in the 1920s. All these changes, he said, should be preceded by price reform.

Other Soviet economists, for example, Anikin (1989), Doronin (1988) and Kuznetsov (1988), suggested the establishment of an exchange market that would be restricted to residents. Nikolai Petrakov proposed the introduction of a realistic exchange rate before price reforms (in contrast to Aganbegyan). Anikin argued that "if any real form of convertibility is introduced it can only function under the system of a more or less stable exchange rate. To ensure this relative stability the state has to effect regulations and market intervention which presupposes the existence of sufficient foreign exchange reserves and/or access to money market including probably the support on the part of the I.M.F." (1989, p. 3). In an article published in 1989, Konstantinov argued that currency convertibility is an "objective necessity" (p. 33). In principle, his plan resembles the Aganbegyan proposal.

This brief discussion indicates that Eastern European policymakers and scholars agree that convertibility should be introduced, but they see the road to convertibility as a rather long one (although they all are optimistic about future prospects). The answer to the question of how to introduce it and what the starting point should be are obviously difficult macroeconomic, but also political, questions. A cautious approach in the reforming countries with their many economic (including the lack of large convertible currency reserves), political, and social problems is obviously on their political agenda. Some scholars also suggest such an approach. Dornbusch states that "if the margin for error in an immediate move to convertibility is very high, it is better that the change happens more slowly. Full convertibility in three years is better than a reaction against quick action which leads to trade restrictions and inconvertibility for a long time to come."[3] The policy approach in the individual Eastern European countries depends on the specific type of policy reform they have in mind and on the specific political, economic and social conditions. However, the Eastern European countries are making a careful analysis of the relative advantages and disadvantages of implementing such policies, given their wide-ranging implications for economic and political life.[4]

NECESSITY AND ADVANTAGES
OF CONVERTIBILITY

Why is the problem of achieving convertibility so important in light of the present economic reforms in Eastern Europe? What are the advantages of convertibility? The principal answer to these questions was briefly discussed in the previous chapters. Here I will summarize the main advantages of convertibility.

Let me begin with the three reasons why a foreign partner accepts and holds domestic currency: as a vehicle currency for trade transactions; as a store of value; and for intervention purposes in order to maintain a fixed exchange rate. Thus, achieving the convertibility of the Eastern European currencies has three main advantages:

First, it will be a powerful instrument for promoting economic efficiency in the inefficient economies that are attempting to transform themselves into market economies. The experience of many industrialized and developing countries has shown that the main advantage of introducing and maintaining convertibility (mainly on the current account) derives from the impact it has on the structure of the economy and on the domestic market. Specifically, it puts pressure on inefficient sectors to adjust and thus achieve structural changes that will lead to a pattern of production that is competitive on foreign markets. It will also reduce domestic price distortions and allow prevailing foreign prices to have a direct impact on the domestic price structure. In other words, convertibility will strengthen the linkages between domestic and external financial and commodities markets.

Second, it will facilitate rapid integration of the Eastern European economies into the existing global world system of trade and payments.

Third, it may allow the Eastern European countries to finance their trade largely in their own currencies, thus allowing the countries to run a trade deficit without having to settle the balance in the currency of their trading partners.

The key reason is, of course, the first one, while the third one, the idea that it will reduce the Eastern European countries' financing needs (given the large external debt and trade deficits with Western countries), is illusory, at least in the short- and medium-term period after convertibility is introduced. Very few convertible currencies are vehicle currencies for trade, and it will take time to persuade foreign partners about the usefulness of holding Eastern European currencies as well as about the Eastern Europeans' willingness or ability to honor their commitments. Creating confidence in the stability of the Eastern European policies will be very important in this respect.

Eastern Europe obviously considers these to be advantages of convertibility as demonstrated by the economic policies of these countries in 1990–92. In early 1990 the president of the Hungarian National Bank emphasized that "convertibility is an instrument that should be used to create a competitive and efficient economy" (*New York Times*, 6 March 1990, p. D7). Soviet economist Anikin stated:

The considerations put forward in favour of convertibility are of an economic and of a social policy nature. It is in line with the principles of the economy which it is intended to set up as a result of the consistent pursuit of the reforms. . . . The closure of the economy, the isolation of enterprises from the fresh breezes of competition and from the world market favour the retention of backwardness, hinder technical progress, weaken incentives to improving the quality and reliability of manufactures. Convertibility is organically inherent in the market economy as a mechanism for linking the internal and external markets. By creating the possibility for enterprises to choose markets on which to buy and sell, it promotes optimization of their activity and improves the industries' efficiency. At the level of social policy convertibility is in line with the idea of integrating the USSR into world society and creates favourable, normal conditions for developing cultural, touristic and other contacts and ensuring individual contacts among people (1989a, pp. 10–11).

There are some specific advantages of introducing convertibility in Eastern Europe. As Sachs points out, since the smaller former CMEA countries are close to Western Europe, convertibility will provide "an immediate source of strong competition for the state enterprises" (1990, p. 22); the access of Eastern Europe to Western short- and long-term capital (loans, securities, etc.) will increase; and Eastern Europe will be in a position to establish flexible trade relations in international markets.

PRELIMINARY CONDITIONS FOR THE INTRODUCTION OF CONVERTIBILITY

The introduction and maintenance of convertibility are associated with substantive modifications of the economic mechanism in every country. This is relevant for the industrialized or developing market economies. In the case of the Eastern European countries with their large state sector (in industry), the necessary modifications of the economic mechanism and economic policy play an important role in the successful implementation of the removal of exchange controls and the change of the currency status (which seems to be a quite simple act from a legal point of view).

What are the preliminary conditions for introducing convertibility?

To answer this question, we must begin with the consideration that convertibility occurs when there are no restrictions on the use, holding or exchange of the currency. The answer could be very brief: create a market. However, the answer to the question of *how* to eliminate the restrictions on the use, holding or exchange of the currency is a very important part of the much more difficult question of *how* to transform the centrally planned economies into market economies. As was stated earlier, the question is beyond the scope of the present study. The focus in this section is therefore on the main preliminary macroeconomic conditions.

As Allen points out, "convertibility is not a gimmick that can be achieved through sophisticated financial engineering and which suddenly brings benefits to the economy" (1990, p. 14). The most important condition for its introduction in Eastern Europe is the existence of a real market (consumer goods, raw materials and intermediate goods, capital goods, capital assets, and financial instruments) in these countries. Convertibility is not a precondition for creating a market but a consequence of it. Moreover, convertibility per se will not resolve Eastern Europe's present economic problems. The inconvertibility (commodity and currency) in the centrally planned economies in Eastern Europe from the 1950s until the early 1990s was a result of central planning and allocation of resources, leading to a "shortage" economy. Convertibility and central planning are incompatible. Radical market-oriented reforms of the price, exchange rate, monetary and fiscal policies, and market-oriented institutional changes in the financial and banking system (competing banks, stock exchange, etc.) are the principal answers to the currency convertibility problem in Eastern Europe.

The approach to convertibility also requires a clearly defined national development strategy as well as clearly defined export strategies and economic growth policies. In the smaller Eastern European countries, the changing political and economic relations between East and West require the implementation of an economic development strategy that considers relations with the Western countries (and in particular Western Europe, the United States, and Japan), the former Soviet Union and the former CMEA region.

What are the obstacles? The main obstacle is the existence of excess demand in the continuing "shortage" and recessionary economies in Eastern Europe. The recent two years of radical economic reforms have revealed a serious danger of creating an inflationary spiral, which means that the allocation of goods may be as distorting as in the past, since the effect of the inflationary spiral on the distribution of power to spend is fairly arbitrary.

What specific institutional and monetary conditions are needed to introduce convertibility?

- Bringing the budget deficit into equilibrium in all the Eastern European countries. The budget deficit, which in Poland and Russia reached 7 to 9 percent of GDP, is a serious obstacle to implementing domestic price reform (wholesale and retail prices).

- Liberalizing trade. Trade liberalization, in the absence of budget deficit equilibrium, would result in a huge increase of imports at any exchange rate, thus exacerbating the external balance problem of Eastern Europe.

- Establishing a realistic and unified exchange rate. The Eastern European currencies were overvalued for more than four decades.[5] The system of currency auctions in the former Soviet Union, Poland, Bulgaria, the former Czechoslovakia and Romania, as was mentioned earlier in this chapter, was a first step in the direction of a realistic rate (as well as an embryonic form of "domestic" financial convertibility). The exchange rates must be realistic and competitive, considering also their plans to be associated with the European Community and to join the European Monetary Union. As John Williamson points out, Eastern Europe cannot expect to receive financial relief whether or not it is entering a monetary union, and these countries must make sure that their exchange rates remain competitive: "Monetary union is too much of a risk at this stage."[6] Serious consideration should also be given to the floating exchange rate practices in the postcommunist economies, particularly those in the early stages of introducing currency convertibility. Certainly, a fixed exchange rate regime promotes stability as well as socially and politically more acceptable wage policies and living standards.

- Eliminating primitive trading practices such as barter in the domestic economy and thus creating the basis for commodity convertibility.

- Eliminating political intervention and administrative controls in economic processes; that is, reducing the power of the old bureaucratic structures.

- Stabilizing the external balance, which involves (1) reducing the external debt burden and at least the short-term obligations to foreigners (since holding large short-term claims by nonresidents makes the country vulnerable to sudden shifts of sentiment); (2) accumulating foreign exchange reserves although if the country is creditworthy, it will have an access to lines of credit, including IMF funds; and

(3) mobilizing a large exportables sector (e.g., through joint ventures, free trade zones) and stimulating foreign direct and equity investments (e.g., providing legal certainty, clear allocation of responsibilities, infrastructure). Among the alternatives that might be considered is introducing "parallel" currency in the free trade zones and limited convertibility (commodity and currency) for nonresidents, using the "shadow" exchange rate as a commercial unified exchange rate.[7]

This list of preliminary conditions is not exhaustive, and the order in which they are listed is not indicative of their order of importance. All of them are important, and all of them are conditional one on the other.

One important institutional problem presently troubling Eastern Europe is the inability of their central banks to effectively control inflation. In addition, they do not have de facto independence from the government and effective bank regulation policies. In Russia, for example, the so-called Central Bank has been printing rubles in ever increasing numbers and denominations and is even trying to keep up with the demand for them in the enterprises. A recent report of the RFE/RL (Vol. 1, No. 23, 5 June 1992) discusses the crisis in the banking system of Poland, where large state-owned commercial banks control the provision of credit in the country by supporting mainly the old communist network and not the private sector. These banks do not have a policy that would force inefficient state enterprises to restructure themselves or to declare bankruptcy. A great number of these state commercial banks are themselves bankrupt. As some reports suggest, between one-fifth and one-third of their assets may be worthless (*The Economist*, 23 January 1993, p. 15). The inefficient state industry sector, which at present does not contribute to the growth of the domestic economy, is undermining the entire banking system; consequently the process of transformation has been hurt both economically and politically.

Another problem is the large number of small banks, the majority of which were established on the basis of the former Central Bank branches. These banks were set up in haste without serious evaluation, although their aim—to transform the banking system and make it more efficient—was a noble one. The banks are also undercapitalized, with few deposits and risk portfolios, and they perform mainly regional operations. The same situation holds for all the Eastern European countries. Not everyone would agree with this assessment. Officials from the Central Bank of Bulgaria (Bulgarian National Bank), for example, stated in 1992 that the Central Bank would not meet any new requirements from the minister of finance for new funds, other than the previously agreed limit, until the end of 1992. This did not prove to be true *ex-ante*. Also, it is doubtful that in the future such an independent policy can be the de facto policy of the Central Bank.

Even in some developed economies the Central Bank is not independent. Very few developing countries, Chile and Colombia, for example, established independent central banks in the 1980s. Although some of the Eastern European countries (Bulgaria, the former Czechoslovakia and Hungary) passed laws affecting their central bank institutions in 1991–92, based on the regulations for the *Deutsche Bundesbank*, it will obviously take some time for them to begin to "imitate" the strong anti-inflationary policies of the German central bank.

Improving the efficiency of the banking system in postcommunist Europe is very important because banks are the main financial intermediary in the economy, inasmuch as the countries have no well-functioning stock and bond markets or venture capital firms. The Central Banks must further develop their principal functions of refinancing commercial banks, managing the country's re- serves, serving as fiscal agent of the state and acting as the bank supervisory institution. Bank supervision seems to be a very important issue vis-à-vis improving the overall efficiency of the country's banking system. Also important is the complex issue of the political accountability of the Eastern European Central Banks.

Confidence in the national currencies obviously depends on maintaining monetary stability. The precondition for a successful transition toward convertibility is the creation of a stable monetary situation both internally and externally. One of the Central Bank's main objectives is to independently determine and strictly monitor the money supply and lending in the domestic economy. In the former Soviet Union, the Central Bank should exercise this kind of control in the entire ruble area. It must therefore clarify with the other republics' central banks the extent to which they will have access to the currency, which also implies the coordination of economic policies. It remains to be seen, however, whether there will actually be a unified economic area that uses the ruble as the common currency. Such a large economic area would no doubt provide certain advantages, not only facilitating the flow of goods, services and capital but also freeing the individual republics of having to develop their own monetary and exchange rate policies. It is by no means clear, however, whether the republics would be prepared to renounce part of their sovereignty, especially in light of their fierce rejection of any kind of Russian neocolonial predominance.

The large interenterprise debt in all the Eastern European countries is another critical issue connected with currency stability and convertibility. At some point, this problem replaced the "monetary overhang" question of households and firms in the late 1980s and 1990. The informal expansion of the credit supply in the economy has softened the tight money and credit policies of the Central Banks. The adopted strategy in some of these countries (e.g., Bulgaria, Russia) to write off the debts or to issue government bonds guaranteeing repayments in the future (e.g., ten- to fifteen-year period) is obviously plausible, considering the present danger of inflationary pressures. As John Williamson has observed, the *real* problem today in Russia is the hyperinflation (*Financial Times*, 25 August 1992, p. 10).

With regard to wage policy, MIT economist Stanley Fischer has stated that

partial but not full wage indexation is desirable; this should be seen as a trade off between reducing the adverse consequences of inflation for workers and social peace, and preventing hyper-inflation. Progressive taxation of wage increases above the norm helps prevent management

from decapitalizing firms in collaboration with workers, and also helps
slow a wage-price spiral (1992, p. 37).

Former finance minister and architect of the "big bang" program
for Poland, Leszek Balcerowicz, made the same statement at his
public lecture in Harvard in March 1992.

As stated in Chapters 2–4, tight monetary policy is part of the
present stabilization program in the region. However, a certain
easing of interest rate policies is required in order to give these
economies a chance to take off. The recession is so deep that further
tightening of interest rate policies would be counterproductive. In
this regard, I should mention that even in Germany the tight
monetary policies of the Deutsche Bundesbank were criticized in
July 1992 in a study of the German Institute for Economic Research
(DIW). The German Central Bank was accused of pursuing a
misguided and self-defeating tight monetary policy, which threat-
ens to undermine the entire restructuring process in East Germany
(*Financial Times*, 30 July 1992, p. 2). Some easing of the monetary policy finally occurred in early 1993.

The above discussion points to the conclusion that measures to
stabilize the domestic economy to establish financial discipline
and to restore equilibrium are of crucial importance for the introduction of convertibility. Timing will play a very serious role in
this respect. Currency convertibility should be introduced not too
early or too late. All the measures discussed above should be
introduced simultaneously and at the "right moment," considering
the specific political, economic and social conditions that obtain
in the individual Eastern European countries and, of course, their
strategy to achieve convertibility. If, however, the government
delays the introduction of some policies (e.g., budget deficit policies), it may lose economic control. Later, political and social
considerations may make it infeasible to introduce and implement
successful stabilization policies because the "timing" would be
wrong (e.g., elections, social unrest). If the government introduces
convertibility too early, for the same reasons it might be forced to

retreat from such a policy and to impose instead some other measures (e.g., increased export taxes).

SCENARIOS FOR ACHIEVING CONVERTIBILITY IN EASTERN EUROPE

What can be done to achieve convertibility? What should be done?

Although a clear-cut answer to these complex questions is not possible, it is obvious that the introduction of currency convertibility is an integral part of economic reform in Eastern Europe and the transformation into market economies and democracies. As domestic markets are created and freed, producers and suppliers are driven by these markets, and trade is liberalized, conditions for currency convertibility will be created.

Achieving convertibility is one of the key goals of reform and one of the most serious tools for integrating Eastern Europe into the world system of trade and payments. Therefore, a more rapid move toward convertibility will be of great advantage for Eastern Europe. However, as stated earlier, introducing financial convertibility in the absence of successful economic reform will have an adverse impact. Both financial and commodity convertibility have to be created. In a situation of zig-zag policies of economic reform, financial convertibility for nonresidents would be to a large extent meaningless if the conditions discussed in the previous section were not achieved. In such a situation, financial convertibility for residents would also be meaningless because without commodity convertibility and the existence of "shortage" economies, a country would rapidly run on the foreign exchange reserves, or the exchange rate would go into free fall.

As noted earlier, the principal approach to introducing currency convertibility for both residents and nonresidents depends on the individual country's development strategy and reform program, but there are no such programs in the region. Obviously, convertibility will be very advantageous if it can take place in a stable macroeconomic environment. The approach to currency convertibility therefore depends on the progress of the economic reform process as well as on East-West political and economic relations.

Developments in Eastern Europe during 1990–92 showed that the principal approaches to transforming the economy and introducing convertibility could be gradual ones or could be achieved through a "shock" to the economy, with the concomitant risk of retreat from such policies and trade restrictions and inconvertibility in the future. Here I briefly discuss four scenarios for achieving convertibility based on present developments and on the successful developments in postwar Western Europe.

The "Shock" Scenario

I begin with a scenario that I will call "Sachs's scenario" or a "shock scenario" because it is based on the economic stabilization program introduced and implemented in Poland in January 1990 and in large part proposed by the Harvard professor Jeffrey Sachs.

The Sachs scenario consists of four parts (Sachs, 1990, p. 22):

1. Introduce market-clearing prices determined in part on free trade with the West.
2. Establish and enlarge the private sector by removing administrative restrictions.
3. Increase the control and financial discipline ("hard budget constraint") over the large state sector by privatization and bankruptcy regulations.
4. Maintain overall macroeconomic stability through restrictive monetary and fiscal policies.

As Sachs emphasizes,

Convertibility has long seemed a distant dream to many economists in Eastern Europe, yet it can be accomplished rapidly through sharp devaluation combined with restrictive macroeconomic policies and financial control over state enterprises. Since the Eastern European countries are small economies close to Western Europe, open trade will provide an immediate source of strong competition for the state enterprises. . . . It is crucial to establish the principles of free trade, currency convertibility and free entry to business early in the reform process (1990, pp. 22–23).

Convertibility of the currency for residents and nonresidents was seen as the first step, followed by the introduction of new tax regulations, privatization schemes and trade reform (Sachs, 1990a, p. 27). Convertibility and a realistic, uniform market-clearing exchange rate create the conditions for the liberalization of imports, and all agents in the economy conduct imports freely. Sachs's plan emphasizes that "at the new exchange rate anyone who wants foreign exchange for current account transactions should be able to obtain it" (Sachs and Lipton, 1989, p. 3). (In my judgment, at the beginning of the stabilization program under the "shock" scenario, certain regulations should be imposed. Only the private sector should be allowed to obtain foreign exchange for imports, since in a situation in which the excess demand from the large state sector is not under an effective financial discipline, it would not be plausible to allow it full freedom to import.)

The key part of the shock scenario is the rapid establishing of currency convertibility. According to Sachs and Lipton, "Creating a unified and convertible exchange rate will be the single most important reform of the Polish economic system" (1989, p. 1). The advantages are, first, restoring confidence in the national currency (which technically could be achieved by a fixed parity backed by an adequate level of foreign exchange reserves); second, reducing the budget deficit and strengthening the monetary policy (as a result partly of the exchange rate unification and the corresponding relative price adjustments in the economy, which will eliminate the need for substantial export subsidy schemes, and others); and third, linking the domestic economy with the international markets and thus improving efficiency through the unified exchange rate, which will provide strong competition for domestic agents. Depreciation of the exchange rate will raise prices P and will lower real money balances M/P, leading to the tightening of monetary policy. For Eastern European countries like Poland with high inflationary pressure and foreign currency cash, the liquidity squeeze will help reduce the monetary overhang and convert existing foreign currency assets.

In implementing the Sachs scenario, the changes of relative prices can be expected to lead to the appearance of new entrepreneurs. But if a country has only a few main export items (e.g., coal, oil, and gas), then the government must strongly encourage *potential* producers and exporters (e.g., through tax policy).

The part of the stabilization program that involves free trade is very important. In this connection, we should recall the words Keynes wrote about free trade almost sixty years ago: "I believe in free trade because in the long run and in general it is the only policy which is technically sound and intellectually tight" (1963, p. 326). However, since the 1930s, many government officials and policymakers have accepted the notion of liberalizing economic life and trade, much as Churchill accepted the notion of democracy as a state organization and political philosophy. Recent experiences show that economic and trade liberalization in many developing countries has followed changes in political regime (South Korea and Chile) or economic crisis (Bolivia, Mexico, Vietnam).

The Sachs scenario can largely be associated with the devaluation/anti-inflationary packages known as the IMF stabilization programs, aimed at import and export liberalization, which will lead to an improved balance between domestic supply and demand and a strengthened balance of payments. Trade liberalization and devaluation of overvalued exchange rates were at the core of the successful outward-oriented development strategies of the newly industrialized countries in Southeast Asia in the 1970s and 1980s. As Krueger points out in her analysis of South Korea, Turkey, Chile, Brazil and other developing countries,

The reduction in the extent of import substitution can lead to an improvement in export performance. . . . The liberalization played a major role through bias reduction, and it was the latter which was really the key variable in determining export behaviour. In turn, export performance was the major mechanism by which the consequences of the devaluation package were transmitted to economic growth (1978, p. 298).

The shock scenario was introduced during 1990–92 in almost all the Eastern European countries. It requires a combination of political and social factors that favor its introduction and successful implementation. We might speculate that the former communist government of Poland, for example, would not have been able to introduce such a stabilization program. In 1990, the Solidarity government had extensive social support for economic policies associated with "shock" to the economy and aimed at rapidly establishing stable macroeconomic environment.

The high social costs associated with such a scenario are not politically sustainable over a long period of time, a point that scholars, economists and politicians should give serious thought to in any reform plan. Political and social issues are not externalities in the reform but are at the heart of its agenda. In such a situation, not just those policies that "make sense" from an economic point of view should be considered as reform strategies.

Gradualist Scenarios

Gradual approaches to the introduction of convertibility are obviously preferred in Eastern Europe at present. I will discuss three such scenarios.

Europe today is divided into four groups of countries: the Western European members of the European Community; the neutral Western European countries; the smaller Eastern European countries (former CMEA Five); and the former Soviet Union. With respect to currency convertibility, the European countries are divided into two groups: Western countries with convertible currencies and Eastern European countries with nonconvertible currencies or with limited currency convertibility.

Changes in East-West relations and discussions in the West, particularly in Western Europe, about integrating Eastern Europe into the Western system of trade and payments and about supporting the transformation of their economies and societies into democracies, raise the question of whether past experience in liberalizing trade and payments in postwar Europe remains relevant for unifying European economic life, or for an OECD multilateral system in which Eastern Europe is included.

Such a scenario can be called a gradualist scenario because the achievement of multilateralism, transferability and convertibility will be a gradual process. Support for the idea of multilateralism is very strong in the West today, and such a scenario could be the best method not only for solving the convertibility problem in Eastern Europe, but also for effecting the smooth transformation of their economies into market-oriented economies.

Next I present the general idea for creating a multilateral system incorporating Eastern Europe in the framework of Europe (the European Community) and the OECD, without discussing details of the specific institutional mechanism of such arrangements.

European Payments System Scenario
(Gradualist Scenario I)

The idea for the European Payments System (EPS) scenario is based on the assumption that the Western European countries and particularly the EC will adopt a new Economic Recovery Program for Eastern Europe. Other Western European countries actively involved in East-West trade like Austria, Switzerland and Scandinavia might be expected to be interested in joining such a program as well. The European Payments System can help Eastern Europe to move from bilateralism (both within Eastern Europe and with the Western countries) to convertibility and to the global European market. Such an approach is to a great extent in accord with the plans for the post–1992 European Community.

The principal component of the EPS scenario is the creation of a European Clearing System. The idea for a multilateral clearing system as a mechanism for promoting multilateral trade and payments is not a new one. Keynes suggested such a system shortly after the war between Germany and the Soviet Union began in

1941; he proposed the establishment of an International Clearing Union as a key approach to a postwar policy toward establishing a free and multilateral international economic system. Indeed, the creation of the Bretton Woods institutions in 1944 was inspired by the Keynes concept.

As Diebold (1952) and Kaplan and Schleiminger (1989) state in their analyses, the subsequent postwar European Payments Union (EPU) was similar to the concept proposed by Keynes. However, it was different in two main aspects: (1) It was a regional, rather than a global, system, and (2) it created much less international credit and played a much more important role for periodic settlements in gold or U.S. dollars. It was similar to the Keynes concept in that it provided for the automatic clearing of payments between central banks for all current account transactions, and it also provided for freely transferable currencies, which was Keynes's key approach to moving toward free multilateral trade and payments. After eight years of EPU life, by 1958 all Western European currencies were made freely convertible into dollars, which was an important preliminary step in establishing broader international financial relations. As many analysts point out, the EPU was an innovative institutional framework through which Western Europe with American help recovered from the Second World War, eliminated bilateralism and import restrictions (dating back to the 1930s) and introduced currency convertibility (first on the trade account and the current account, and later gradually removed most of the restrictions on the capital account). It was also the basis for unprecedented economic growth and prosperity in Western Europe. Its experience suggests the desirability of extending the scope of international policy coordination beyond crisis management.

The EPU's economic and political philosophy and its institutional mechanism are analyzed in Diebold (1952), Kaplan and Schleiminger (1989) and other works. Here I will briefly discuss some EPU institutional arrangements that could provide the basis for similar arrangements in the framework of the EPS scenario. The EPU was set up in 1950 by the members of the Organization for European Economic Cooperation (OEEC) and was partly supported by the Marshall Plan. The multilateral settlements were arranged in the framework of cooperation between the EPU, the OEEC and the Bank for International Settlements (BIS). The monthly compensations and settlements were carried out principally in the BIS which also operated as an EPU Central Bank. In order to save liquidity (which is also a serious problem for the Eastern European countries at present), the EPU system provided for the offsetting of the countries' monthly bilateral surpluses and deficits with each other, which required settling only the country's net surplus or deficit with the rest of the EPU members (taken together). The national currencies of the EPU countries were freely transferable between one another, insofar as they were held at central banks' accounts. The individual countries' monthly settlements of their net position with the rest of the EPU members were made partly through the provision and taking of credit, which stimulated the process of trade liberalization within Europe and saved foreign exchange reserves.

The balance-of-payments adjustment was achieved by setting quota limits for each country and by making cash settlements (in U.S. dollars and gold). In the first years of the EPU, these settlements increased progressively since deficit members made cumulative use of their quota facilities. An important policy arrangement within the EPU system was the introduction of stabilization programs, similar to the IMF stabilization programs, with conditional provisions of funds for countries with balance-of-payments difficulties (e.g., Germany in 1951). At the same time, surplus countries were urged to limit their surpluses through import liberalization and through the provision of credit. Close macroeconomic policy coordination and adjustment of policies toward balance within the system was the principal approach to trade multilateralism, transferability and, subsequently, currency convertibility in Europe in the 1950s.

The EPU was established only six years after the Bretton Woods Agreement and with the assistance of the United States. The parallel existence of these two multilateral financial systems (regional and global) did not prove to contradict in principle each other's policies. During the existence of the EPU, the United States had a pragmatic attitude toward trade diversion.

The European Payments System scenario could lead to the convertibility of the Eastern European currencies within three to five years (or even earlier), given the now favorable political and economic conditions for East-West cooperation. All of the Eastern European countries (the Eastern Europe Six, together with the new Slovak republic, and some of the former Soviet republics, such as the Baltics) would be interested in participation. The smaller Eastern European countries such as Bulgaria and Poland had some experiences (though limited) as democracies and market economies in the period between the two world wars. The "gradualist" scenario could provide the best framework for the revival of these potential new democracies. It will also create a favorable basis for stimulating regional economic relations.

Policies could be coordinated through the European Community. The monthly multilateral settlements and compensations (similar to the EPU scheme) could be carried out through BIS in Basle, which operates as an EPS Central Bank. (The Eastern European countries, including the former Soviet Union, have some traditional contacts, most of whom are members of BIS; BIS was actively involved in resolving the liquidity crisis in Hungary in early 1982). The balance-of-payments adjustments could be achieved through a combination of a quota system and cash settlements (in ECU and gold). Russia would probably favor the introduction of gold in the cash settlements because it has considerable gold reserves. The automatic settlement scheme should urge the Western European countries to import liberalization.

Coordination of policies in the EPS (including central bank coordination) and stabilization programs for countries with balance-of-payments difficulties will be essential to the success of gradualist scenario I. Policy advice to Eastern Europe on fiscal and monetary policies and on supporting measures, such as trade liberalization, debt repayment and freeing of capital movements, should be done on a regular basis. Debt-relief measures for some Eastern European countries could also be considered (as in the case of Germany in 1953). Therefore, the EPS could lend great support to the economic reform process in Eastern Europe. However, the success of the EPS scenario will to a great extent depend on the determination of Eastern European governments to adopt market-oriented economic reforms and democratic societies, as well as on their political will to trade and cooperate with each other. Achieving some kind of macroeconomic equilibrium in the East European economies is another important condition. The social cost of adjustment will probably be less than in the Sachs scenario. The EPS scenario will help lead to gradual integration of all the Eastern European countries into today's global international financial system.

OECD Payments System Scenario (Gradualist Scenario II)

The approach to gradually integrating Eastern Europe into the world system of trade and payments and to the convertibility of the Eastern European currencies could also be considered within the more complex (and probably institutionally more difficult for implementation) framework of the present OECD system, incorporating not only the Western European countries but also the United States, Japan, Canada and Australia. This scenario can be called the OECD Payments System scenario. Since all industrial countries are considering programs of assistance to Eastern Europe, including the other major industrialized countries in an Economic Recovery Program for Eastern Europe would be very desirable. The former Soviet Union, for example, has stated many times that it is eager to expand economic cooperation with Japan in the Far East. Japan, with its huge trade and current account surpluses, could be one of the major creditors, if not the major creditor, given the potential increased credit demand in Germany in connection with German reunification. The multilateral settlements and compensations could operate much as in the EPS scenario. The BIS could be the agent for the monthly payments settlements. Policies within the system could be coordinated through the OECD or through a new organization called, for example, the Organization for Economic Reconstruction. The cash settlements are made in U.S. dollars (the currency of the system's major trade nation) and gold.

Eastern European Payments System Scenario (Gradualist Scenario III)

Since 1990, many discussions and conferences have been held, and book volumes published, on the issue of creating a multilateral payments system, including the former Eastern European countries; only the smaller ones; or only the former Soviet Union, or both. Intellectually, it is an interesting proposal, but whether it is politically viable is a matter for another discussion. As Dornbusch states, "the West can capitalize and guarantee the mechanism" (1992, p. 22), and it can administer the system. He also points out that in the case of the 1950 European Payments Union (EPU), the United States contributed capital of $270 million, and, as some estimates suggest, equivalent funding today would require $1.8 billion. Obviously, the latter financial requirement does not present a serious financial burden, if we consider that for only the stabilization and support of the ruble convertibility in the present hyperinflation situation in Russia, a fund of $6 billion is needed (in the optimistic scenario).

The idea of using convertible currencies for part of the settlements (or for all of them) in the Eastern European multilateral system seems to be attractive. Such a system would certainly give the "deficit" members an incentive to balance their accounts. However, we should consider the tension in the overall Eastern European external balance (huge external debt) in convertible currencies. As Holzman notes in respect to the former CMEA: "until CMEA is in some kind of hard-currency equilibrium with the West it would not seem possible to use hard currencies to multilateralize intra-CMEA trade since at least one partner will always insist on a bilateral balance" (1978, p. 161).

A possible scenario for solving this dilemma would be to provide Western aid (as in the EPU scenario) or loans to the reforming Eastern European countries (which give part of it to the common funds), and some debt-relief schemes for their convertible currency debt in the West.

Whether such a scenario has a future is difficult to predict. Success depends heavily on the overall political climate in East-West relations and on the political will of former CMEA countries to cooperate with each other. However, there is no doubt that, despite some policy contradictions the Western countries are considering increasing their financial assistance (loan and aid) to Eastern Europe, including the former Soviet Union.

The Eastern European Payments System scenario for the introduction of convertibility differs a great deal from the Sachs scenario. Sachs states that "the answers to Eastern Europe's needs lie mainly in integration with Western Europe, whose market is perhaps 15 times as large" as the Eastern European market (1990, p. 25). This statement gives a reason for some comparisons with the prewar period. Before the Second World War, foreign trade within the area of the present countries of Central and Eastern Europe was relatively small—about 15 percent of the total—while that with the Soviet Union was negligible. Trade was directed westward, largely toward Germany, the United Kingdom and the United States (Dewar, 1951, p. 1).

Sachs also states that Eastern European integration as a precursor of integration with the world economy will be simply a "poor man's club" (1990, p. 26) if it does not accelerate but simply tries to replace what will occur naturally if all Eastern European countries apply the shock scenario.

While such a comparison would be helpful, we should consider that the transformation of the Eastern European economies and the approach to the convertibility issue both depend on the political, social and economic conditions in the individual countries. The

Eastern European scenario for convertibility may minimize the risks and difficulties involved in adopting a market orientation and achieving integration into the global economy.

Economic reforms in Eastern Europe and the completely new framework of East-West relations require rapid action to introduce the convertibility of their currencies. The ability to pursue such economic reforms and the stability of this process are very important for the market orientation of the Eastern European countries. Sustained policies for structural adjustment and privatization for eliminating excess demand, improving supply elasticities and price structure, reducing budget deficits and monetary overhang and boosting export performance are urgently needed in order to create the conditions for convertibility. The approach to the convertibility problem ("what can be done" and "what should be done") in the individual countries will depend on their specific political, economic and social situation, as well as on the government's development strategy. The principal approach could be either a rapid move associated with shock to the economy or a gradual transformation. Western financial assistance, particularly in the proposed scenarios for the European Payments System and the OECD Payments System and the Eastern European Payments System, will be essential.

INTERNATIONAL SUPPORT IN THE TRANSITION TO CONVERTIBILITY IN EASTERN EUROPE

The stability of the Eastern European policies aimed at creating market economies and democracies, and the above described schemes for their integration into the regional and global systems of trade and payments, will require some debt-relief measures for Eastern Europe. In this regard, I should note the statement Keynes made in his book *The Economic Consequences of Peace*: "to pay debts . . . [would] certainly be to impose a crushing burden. They [the debtors] may be expected therefore to make constant attempts to evade or escape payments and these attempts will be a constant source of international friction and ill-will for many years to come" (1988 [1919], p. 181).

As historical experience shows (e.g., Germany in the EPU in 1953), debt-relief measures could provide the basis for rapid economic recovery. Eastern Europe has the potential for economic recovery, given its traditional links with Europe and its highly skilled population. Introducing rational and pragmatic economic development strategies at the "right moment," without delay, combined with stable political and economic relations with the West, could provide the climate for the "newly industrialized countries" in Central and Eastern Europe to emerge by the end of this decade.

Conclusion

This study has discussed the issues of economic reforms, economic development strategies and political changes in Eastern Europe in the 1990s. Undoubtedly, it raises as many questions as it answers. As the Nobel laureate in economics, Robert Solow, states, we economists tend "to answer questions more delicate than our limited understanding of complicated questions will allow. Nobody likes to say 'I don't know.' "[1] The present study has attempted to establish a basis for better understanding of the directions in which economic transformation and political changes in Eastern Europe might be expected to move. There are many issues for further research. For example, what impact will the economic reforms have on domestic political developments? What impact will economic changes have on the ethnic conflicts of the region (since when the economy deteriorates, it is easier to be an emotional nationalist than a rational democrat)? What impact will economic development policy have on resolving the external balance problem? What impact will economic and political changes have on East-West security issues?

The economic transformation in the postcommunist European countries and the political liberalization in the region are processes of ideas and actions, and a Darwinian process of trial and errors. No one could make any precise projections for the future of these countries. The Western democracies have sophisticated economic and political systems, which cannot be easily copied in the former communist region. There are too many challenges for Eastern Europe to be successfully resolved in a decade or even in a generation. The capital stock of the Eastern European economies is obsolete and has to be rebuilt through large investments. Human capital has to adjust by retraining the workforce and by reallocation. Infrastructure capital must be improved and restructured. The spatial structure of the economy and the environment, much of which was destroyed by the "central planners," will also have to be restored and adjusted.

Culture and personal freedom will be important factors in the process of change in the region. A certain danger exists that in some of the Eastern European countries the increasing external and internal tensions may result in the fall of the governments implementing the radical economic reforms, and although these countries will probably remain on the road to transformation, they may find themselves under a new form of authoritarian government or with poorly performing (market-oriented) economies and emerging democratic institutions. In this regard, we should remember the words of Schumpeter: "We always plan too much and always think too little. We walk into our future as we walked into the war, blind-folded" (1942, 1947, p. XI).

In this connection, we can also compare the present situation with that in post–World War I Europe, when new democratic governments sprouted all over Europe and an impartial observer in 1925 might have pronounced the future of capitalism secure. Only a decade later, country after country would succumb to dictatorship. Totalitarian fascism covered the map of Europe, displacing the market economies of an earlier era and raising questions about the future of democracy. As Dornbusch stated in a public lecture in May 1992 regarding the potential danger of the Weimarization of Eastern Europe, "Fascism is around the corner" in these countries. For some, this might seem an exaggeration of the threats to the new democracies, but the legacy of the past must not be forgotten. Again we should turn to Hayek's analysis in his 1946 study, in which he wrote that the Nazi ideology was a revolution against the predominant ideas of the nineteenth century: liberal democracy, national self-determination and laissez-faire economics. And further: "It was to a large extent a revolt of a new-under-privileged class against the labour aristocracy which the industrial labour movement has created, . . . the envy of the unsuccessful professional man, the university trained engineer or lawyer, and of the 'white collared proletariat' in general, . . . against the trade unions whose income was many times theirs" (p. 60).

In Eastern Europe the old communist structures have not been uprooted and the older communists, particularly those from the middle-aged generation, many of whom now feel like a "new-under-privileged" class, might revolt against the changes if conditions continue to deteriorate. Populist slogans will attach to the masses. Developments in Slovakia in 1992 and in Russia in 1993 are good examples of when we contemplate such a scenario. Nonetheless, we can be optimistic.

Generally, Eastern Europe will likely move toward democracy and a market economy and will be associated with Western Europe in the long term. This is admittedly an optimistic outlook and one that draws inspiration from Keynes: "If we consistently act on the optimistic hypothesis, this hypothesis will tend to be realized; whilst by acting on the pessimistic hypothesis we can keep ourselves for ever in the pit of want" (1963, p. VII).

Notes

INTRODUCTION

1. Until 2 October 1990 Eastern Europe denoted Bulgaria, Czechoslovakia, the German Democratic Republic (GDR), Hungary, Poland, Romania and the Soviet Union. In December 1991 the Soviet Union was dissolved, and most of the former Soviet republics joined the Commonwealth of Independent States (CIS). In January 1993 Czechoslovakia was divided into Czech and Slovak republics. Eastern Europe as a distinct geographical area with its own political and reformist identity, of course, no longer includes the former GDR. In this book, the terms *Eastern Europe, postcommunist Europe, CMEA,* and *centrally planned economies* are used interchangeably.

2. It might be interesting to mention here the remark Stalin made before the end of the Second World war, which marked the beginning of the Soviet colonization of Eastern Europe: "Whoever occupies a territory also imposes on it his own social system. Everyone imposes his own social system as far as his army can reach. It cannot be otherwise." As regards the former East Germany, the Soviet dictator stated: "The West will make Western Germany their own, and we shall turn Eastern Germany into our own state" (see Milovan Djilas, *Conversations with Stalin* (New York: Harcourt Brace, 1962), pp. 114, 153; cited in Melvin Croan, "Germany and Eastern Europe" in J. Held, ed., 1992, pp. 345–393, 350, 392).

3. Several interesting studies on the economic changes in Eastern Europe were published after 1989. Some of these publications are Christopher Clague and Gordon C. Rausser, *The Emergence of Market Economies in Eastern*

Europe (Oxford: Basil Blackwell, 1992); Institut Vneshnyi Torgovli i Pro-
mishlenosti, "O Sistemnoi Ekonomicheskoi Reforme v Stranach Bishnevo
SSSR: Chemu Uchit Poslevoennyi Opit Japonii" (translation from Japanese),
(Moscow: March 1992); William S. Kern, ed., *From Socialism to Market
Economy: The Transition Problem* (Kalamazoo, Mich.: W. E. Upjohn Institute
for Employment Research, 1992); Peter Murrell, "Evolutionary and Radical
Approaches to Economic Reform," in *Economics of Planning*, no. 25, 1992,
pp. 79–95; and Jan Kregel, Egon Matzner, and Gernot Grabner, eds., *The
Market Shock* (Vienna: Austrian Academy of Sciences, 1992).
  4. Z. Brzezinski, cited in Sir Geoffrey Howe, "Soviet Foreign Policy under
Gorbachev," *The World Today*, March 1989, pp. 40–45, 44.
  5. Janos Kornai, "Comments on the Papers Prepared in the World Bank
about Socialist Countries," unpublished manuscript, 1984, p. 3.
  6. For example, the Dutch political economist Jos de Beus writes: "Let us
define *political* political economy (PPE) as political economy with an economic approach to the political order especially to the behaviour of the state
(economic policy). PPE differs from political economy (PE) when and because
politics is conceived as an endogenous phenomenon" (Jos de Beus, "Comments
on 'The Decline and Rise of Political Economy' by Bruce Yandle," in *European
Journal of Political Economy*, 6, No. 4 (1990): 563–73, 563).

CHAPTER 1. EASTERN EUROPE ON A ROAD
TOWARD RADICAL CHANGE

  1. For an excellent analysis of these issues, see, for example. J. Held, ed.
(1992).
  2. As an illustration of the development stage, for example, of Bulgaria, I
would like to cite here the observations made by the first United States diplomatic agent Charles M. Dickinson to this country in the early twentieth century:
"It is a fine diversified country. . . . In general intelligence, progressive ideas
and a readiness to examine and seize upon new things, Bulgaria is already far
in advance of Turkey and considerably in advance of Southern Russia. . . . Here
the fact that a thing or method is new excites suspicion and distrust; there the
fact that it is recommended by modern nations commands immediate confidence
and respect" (Marin Pundeff, "Bulgaria," in J. Held, ed., 1992, pp. 65–118, 68).
  3. Sharon L. Wolchek, "Czechoslovakia," in J. Held, ed. (1992), pp. 119–
163, 121. Wolchik stresses the following factors: a relatively high level of
economic development, a large middle class, the absence of a native aristocracy
and a predominantly literate population.
  4. The German economist H. P. Widmaier uses the term *logic of politics*
(*Logik der Politik* und *politische Dialogik*).
  5. The terms *social* and *society* are two of the oldest terms describing

systems of interconnections between human activities. They stem from the Latin *societas*, from *socius*, a personally known fellow or companion.

It might be interesting to note briefly Hayek's analysis of the word "social": "The noun 'society' misleading as it is, is relatively innocuous compared with the adjective 'social,' which has probably become the most confusing expression in our entire moral and political vocabulary" (*The Fatal Conceit: The Errors of Socialism*, in *The Collected Works of F. A. Hayek*, vol. I, ed. by W. W. Bartley, III [London: Routledge, 1988], p. 114). As regards the terms *social rule of law* (in German *sozialer Rechtsstaat*) and *social market economy*, Hayek writes that "while the rule of law and the market are at the start, fairly clear concepts, the attribute "social" empties them of any clear meaning" (ibid., p. 117).

6. For an excellent analysis of these problems in the case of Sweden, see, for example, Eric Lundberg, "The Rise and Fall of the Swedish Model," *Journal of Economic Literature* 23 (March 1985): 1–36.

7. The Keynesian-style policies reflected in the government programs, for example, of the Clinton administration in 1993, in Western Europe, and in Japan, following the deep recessions and unemployment problems consequent to the Reagan-Thatcher economic philosophy of the 1980s. Keynes argued that we can rely on the market mechanism to allocate resources when there is full employment, but the market cannot be depended on to maintain a state of continuously full employment. The "zealous Keynesians" (Joan Robinson's school) on the left claim Keynes's support for their radical view that the problems of the capitalist system are so fundamental that they cannot be solved by the fiscal policy advocated by mainstream Keynesians. The extreme conservatives on the right also claim Keynes's support for arguments that oppose this policy because they regard it as endowing the government with too much discretionary power.

8. For a brief description of the flaws of fiscal, price, monetary and exchange rate policy under central planning in Eastern Europe, see Zloch-Christy (1988), pp. 18–21.

9. For further details and analysis, see, for example, J. Kornai, "The Hungarian Reform Process: Visions, Hopes and Reality," *Journal of Economic Literature* (December 1986): 1687–737 and A. Aslund (1990), pp. 2–8.

10. Aslund suggests the following brief definition: "a system of voluntary exchange of property rights for money" (1990, p. 3).

11. These issues will be discussed in Chapters 2, 3, 4, and 5.

12. Obviously, in order to obtain an aggregate evaluation of the performance of an economic system, some kind of welfare function is required according to which different priorities and criteria will be given appropriate weights. Here, I use the criteria (not ordered by their importance) given by Eidem and Viotti in their 1978 study: level of output, rate of growth of output, composition of output (shares of consumption, investment and military programs); collective

versus individual consumption; efficiency; stability of output, employment, and prices; equity and economic security of the individual; and adaptability to change. See Rolf Eidem and Staffan Viotti, *Economic Systems* (New York: John Wiley & Sons, 1978), p. 95.

13. Samuelson's definition of socialism as an economic system refers rather to the so-called democratic economic order (or *sozialer Rechtsstaat, Sozialstaatsprinzip, Sozialstaat,* and *Rechtsstaat*). In order to avoid confusion with the former socialist countries in Eastern Europe, the term *social democratic economic order* is used in the present study.

14. The prevailing view of the present economic philosophy is that the leading industrial countries (the United States, Western Europe and Japan) have *mixed economies,* because of government intervention and regulations (varying in their scope in the individual countries).

CHAPTER 2. ECONOMIC TRANSFORMATION IN EASTERN EUROPE AND THE FORMER SOVIET UNION

1. As will be discussed later in this chapter, none of the Eastern European countries has a clearly defined vision of the future direction of the economic transformation process. In this sense, it would be an exaggeration to say that these countries have programs for changes.

2. A useful summary of the state of economic reforms (price liberalization, privatization, tax reform, laws, etc.) in the individual Eastern European countries and of the former Soviet republics is presented in *World Economic Outlook* (Washington, D.C.: International Monetary Fund, May 1992), pp. 32–33, 38–39.

3. In the future economic historians will probably identify the process of transformation in Eastern Europe not as a "revolution from above" but as a "revolution from below," beginning at the grass-roots levels—new entrepreneurs, small private firms, farms, and so on.

4. Rudiger Dornbusch, presentation at the National Bureau for Economic Research conference on "Transition in Eastern Europe," Cambridge, Mass., February 1992.

5. M. Bruno (1992) presents an excellent analysis of the recent policies of the five smaller Eastern European countries—Bulgaria, Czechoslovakia, Hungary, Poland, and Romania.

6. Some details on the Russian economic reform introduced in January 1992 are as follows. *Prices* (wholesale and retail) were freed on January 2, and a few months later, subsidies to goods such as bread and milk, and to rents, were cut. *Spending* was also cut, subsidies on most industrial products were reduced or eliminated, and weapons orders were slashed by 85 percent (the optimistic goal being to shrink the budget deficit from 15 percent to 1 percent of GNP).

Taxes include a VAT of 15 percent on food and 28 percent on other goods, and an even heavier levy has been placed on corporate profits and many commercial transactions. *Privatization* plans were to sell off 25 percent of state-owned enterprises and property by the end of 1992. Limited *currency convertibility* (on the current account) was introduced, the ruble was floated against the U.S. dollar, but multiple exchange rates (six) remained (*Business Week*, 24 February 1992, p. 67, and Proceedings of the NBER Conference on "Transition in Eastern Europe," Cambridge, Mass., February 1992). J. Sachs (1992, pp. 19–20) summarizes the main goals of the Russian reform in the short run as follows: financial stabilization, stabilization of the external balance (debt-servicing problems), ruble convertibility, market liberalization, rapid privatization, construction of a social safety net, including unemployment compensation, design of an appropriate industrial policy, including reduction of the scale of the military industrial complex, and its transition to civilian use.

7. However, the Ukrainian Parliament threatened to reintroduce price controls a few months later and disapproved the IMF vision on economic reform in March 1992. (*Financial Times*, 4 March 1992, p. 4).

8. L. J. Liberman and L. M. Freinkman, "Neotloznoe razgosudarstvovanie: a nado li speshit?" in *Serija Ekonomiceskaja*, No. 6, 1991, pp. 42–51, 49.

9. Policymakers in Eastern Europe, especially in Poland, state that they have removed all centrally planned controls. This point was stressed by L. Balcerowicz in his public lecture at Harvard University in March 1992. Obviously, research is needed in order to provide a precise answer to the question of *what* the governments will do if *all* government planning and controls were removed, and *how* they will affect macro- and microeconomic policy. Of interest to this issue is the statement of another Polish scholar made at a public lecture at Harvard University in February 1992: "Nothing changed in Poland and economic policy, and its implementation is like [it was] in the communist time" (Adam Biela, Catholic University, Warsaw). This statement is, of course, overly pessimistic, if, for example, the results of the price reforms, monetary policies and the privatization of small- and medium-scale enterprises are considered; this applies not only to Poland but also to Russia and the other Eastern European countries. (The only exception is probably Romania which still has not clearly defined economic reforms.)

10. Cited in *The Economist*, 23 January 1993, p. 15.

CHAPTER 3. ECONOMIC REFORM AND POLITICAL CHANGE

1. Susan Marie Szasz, cited in V. Klaus, *Dismantling Socialism: A Preliminary Report* (Sydney, Australia: Center for Independent Study, 1991), p. 3.

2. Stephen Fischer-Galati, "Old Wine in New Bottles," in J. Held, ed. (1992), pp. 1–16, 16.
3. Cited in Jos de Beus (1990), p. 8.
4. Ibid.
5. Samuel P. Huntington, "The Change to Change: Modernization, Development, and Politics," *Comparative Politics* 2, No. 3 (April 1971), p. 320.
6. Ibid., p. 316.
7. Cited in Jos de Beus, "Applying First World Political Economy to the Second World's March into Civil Society," manuscript, 1991, Harvard University, p. 2.
8. Victor Perez-Diaz, "The Return of Civil Society" (Cambridge, Mass.: Harvard University Press, forthcoming), pp. 54–56.
9. Alex Pravda, cited in Ljubo Sirc, *What Must Gorbachev Do?* (London: Centre for Research into Communist Economies, March 1989), Occasional Paper 2, p. 23.
10. Radio Free Europe/Radio Liberty Research Report, Vol. 1, No. 19, 8 May 1992, p. 21. For an analysis of the inter-republican and foreign trade in the former Soviet Union, see, for example, C. Senik-Leygonie and G. Hughes, "Industrial Profitability and Trade among the Former Soviet Republics," in *Economic Policy*, No. 15 (October 1992): 354–377, especially 368–377.
11. W. Layton and C. Rist, *The Economic Situation of Austria* (Geneva: League of Nations, 1925), cited in Rudiger Dornbusch, "Lessons from the End of the Austro-Hungarian Empire for the Former Soviet Union Today," manuscript, MIT, August 1992, pp. 30–31. From the historical perspective, Peter Hanak analyzes the political and economic disintegration and disruption after the First World War of the Austro-Hungarian empire's economic unity in Central and Eastern Europe. He writes that the provinces of the empire

had become specialized according to the principle of comparative advantages, sending 70–75 percent of their exports to other provinces within the empire. It was under this economic system that the Bohemian (Czech) textile and glass industries, the Austrian engineering industries, and the Hungarian milling industry became large-scale European institutions. The peace treaties sliced up this efficient economic unit, blocked centuries-old commercial routes, and broke off time-tested and fruitful economic relations. These changes were intensified by the post-war chaos, the disintegration of the empire, the sharp decline in production, and unprecedented inflation.... The Central European countries ... chose the worst possible option: isolation from one another in the effort to achieve the highest possible level of autarky. They dissociated themselves from their former partners, imposing bans on exports and imports, applying high protectionist customs tariffs, and from 1931 on, strict state controls on foreign exchange transactions.... As a result, not only did the previously efficient regional distribution of labor collapse, but the economic strategies of development used by the successor states missed the mark as well. It is quite understandable, therefore, that in the 1930s Hungary, hard-hit by permanent unemployment and the marketing crisis, was attracted to the Lebensraum (economic breathing space) of Hitler's Germany (Peter Hanak, "Hungary 1918–1934," in J. Held, 1992, pp. 119–163, 169–170).

12. Rudiger Dornbusch, "Policies to Move from Stabilization to Growth," in *Proceedings of the World Bank Annual Conference on Development Economics 1990* (Washington, D.C.: World Bank, 1991), pp. 19–48, 21.

13. Ibid., pp. 45–46 n.12.

14. Analysis of the privatization in Eastern Europe is discussed in more detail in Patrick Bolton and Gerard Roland, "Privatization Policies in Central and Eastern Europe," *Economic Policy*, No. 15 (October 1992): 276–309; B. Djelic and J. Sachs, "The Russian Mass Privatization Program," manuscript, Harvard Institute for International Development, January 1993; Maxim Boycko, Andrei Shlefer, Robert W. Visny, "Voucher Privatization," unpublished manuscript, Department of Economics, Harvard University, December 1992; and other sources (see note 3 to the Introduction).

15. The concept of the leasing agreement is "paying for use, not ownership." In the West it became an important source of medium-term finance for industry and commerce after the Second World War; for more details, see Zloch-Christy (1991), p. 67.

16. I benefited on this point from a discussion with J. Berliner.

17. John Williamson, for example, suggests that the alternatives to political democracy with a prosperous market economy, in the case of Russia, are "splintering, or a new authoritarianism, or a frustrated nationalism, or some combination of these" (*Financial Times*, 25 August 1992, p. 10).

18. Daniel Bond, *Trade or Aid? Official Export Credit Agencies and the Economic Development of Eastern Europe and the Soviet Union* (New York, Prague: Institute for East-West Security Studies, 1991), Public Policy Paper 4.

CHAPTER 4. ECONOMIC DEVELOPMENT STRATEGIES

1. It is obviously difficult to come up with a general grouping of countries with relatively similar patterns of development. S. Kuznets, Harvard professor and Nobel laureate in economics, liked to note in his lectures on economic development that there are four groups of countries: developed economies, developing economies, Japan and Argentina. (I owe this remark to J. Sachs.)

2. In Southeast Asia, in contrast to Eastern Europe, the governments are

not burdened by budgetary constraints for social protection, and there are almost
no labor unions to defend the interests of the workers.

CHAPTER 5. CURRENCY CONVERTIBILITY IN
THE POSTCOMMUNIST ECONOMIES

1. This part is based on an earlier version of a study prepared for the U.N.
Economic Commission for Europe, Geneva (Zloch-Christy, 1990).

2. Some interesting studies on currency convertibility in Eastern Europe
were published recently. See, for example, F. D. Holzman, "Moving Toward
Ruble Convertibility," *Comparative Economic Studies* 33, No. 3 (Fall 1991):
3–66; John Williamson, *The Economic Opening of Eastern Europe*, Vol. 31,
Washington, D.C., Institute for International Economics, May 1991;
J.van Brabant, *Integrating Eastern Europe into the Global Economy: Convertibility through Payments Union* (New York, 1991); and G. Bakos, "Japan and
Central Europe: New Subregional Formations and Japan's Presence," manu-
script, Tokyo, October 1992.

3. Rudiger Dornbusch, "Payments Mechanism for Russia and Eastern
Europe," unpublished manuscript, Department of Economics, MIT, Cambridge,
Mass., January 1992.

4. The president of the National Bank of Hungary stated that "we want to
reach convertibility not by devaluations but by a deflationary process" (in
contrast to Poland's policy) (*New York Times*, 6 March 1990, p. D7).

5. Some studies suggest that Eastern European currencies are undervalued
against Western currencies considering their purchasing-power parities (PPP).
This statement is probably true (*The Economist*, 20 June 1991, p. 80).

6. Williamson, *The Economic Opening of Eastern Europe*.

7. The introduction of a "parallel" currency in the free trade zones, however, raises interesting questions. In the present unstable economic situation in
Eastern Europe, financial convertibility for nonresidents might appear to be
meaningless. Nonresidents can hold very little of the "parallel" currency and
therefore would benefit little, or they might attract considerable amounts of the
official currency (as residents defeat domestic currency controls and smuggle
the currency out), which would give rise to many problems, including rapid
devaluation of the official currency. The decision about "parallel" currency
should therefore carefully take into account the conditions of the individual
Eastern European countries.

CONCLUSION

1. Cited in Samuelson (1989), p. 673.

Appendix

Table A.1
Eastern Europe: Output 1992
(in % as compared to 1989 = 100%)

Albania	49
Bulgaria	63
Czecho-Slovakia	78
Hungary	83
Poland	81
Romania	79
Russia	72
Ukraine	71

Note: Data are for GNP or GDP except for the Ukraine which is NMP; 1992 are preliminary estimates.

Source: World Bank and PlanEcon database; own estimates.

Table A.2
Eastern European Convertible-Currency Gross Debt, 1985–92
(millions of U.S. dollars, end-period)

	1985	1986	1987	1988	1989	1990	1991	1992
Bulgaria	2,409	5,075	6,000	7,300	10,220	11,400	12,641	14,007
Czechoslovakia	3,013	4,254	5,300	5,700	7,915	8,100	9,365	11,225
Hungary	11,260	15,086	17,500	16,800	20,390	21,270	22,658	23,894
Romania	6,000	6,395	5,700	4,000	516	1,540	2,651	3,939
Poland	30,204	33,526	37,600	37,300	40,793	48,475	48,412	50,300
Eastern Europe 5	52,886	64,336	72,100	71,100	79,834	90,785	95,727	103,365
Soviet Union	25,193	33,061	38,000	38,000	52,800	56,000	70,000[a]	73,000[a]
CMEA banks	2,500	n.a.	n.a.	n.a.	n.a.	n.a.	n.a.	n.a.
Total	80,579	97,397	110,100	109,100	132,634	146,785	165,727	176,365

[a]Share of Russia ca. 60 percent.

Source: Zloch-Christy (1991), p. 34; PlanEcon Review and Outlook, November 1992; BIS; author's estimates.

Table A.3
Eastern European Convertible-Currency Net Debt, 1985–92
(millions of U.S. dollars, end-period)

	1985	1986	1987	1988	1989	1990	1991	1992
Bulgaria	635	3,694	4,600	6,400	8,849	10,917	11,560	12,744
Czechoslovakia	1,943	3,037	4,000	4,200	5,759	6,998	6,175	8,600
Hungary	9,358	12,898	15,800	15,600	19,144	20,201	18,723	17,894
Romania	5,500	5,760	4,750	2,600	-1,243	1,167	2,328	3,128
Poland	28,606	31,805	35,300	34,050	36,039	40,635	41,907	43,157
Eastern Europe 5	46,042	57,194	64,450	62,850	68,548	79,918	80,693	85,523
Soviet Union	14,545	18,292	24,500	23,500	49,800	53,000	65,000[a]	69,000[a]
CMEA banks	2,500	n.a.	n.a.	n.a.	n.a.	n.a.	n.a.	n.a.
Total	63,087	75,486	88,950	86,350	118,348	132,918	145,693	154,523

[a]Share of Russia ca. 60 percent.

Source: Zloch-Christy (1991), p. 35; PlanEcon Review and Outlook, November 1992; BIS; author's estimates.

Table A.4
Privatization in Hungary
(1991)

	Number of Enterprises	Value of Assets (bn. forints)	Percent of book value of state assets	SPA participation (percent)	Foreign share (percent)
Approved transformations	45	68.7	3.6	64.5	19
Approved associations with foreign participation	40	37.9	2	–	45.3
Approved associations with domestic partners	35	34.7	1.8	–	–
Sales under property protection	54	6	0.3	–	–
First privatization program	20	90.4	4.7	36	42
Pre-privatization	95	0.8	–	–	–

Source: State Property Agency (SPA), Annual Report 1991, Budapest.

Table A.5
Privatization in Poland
(1991)

	Changed into State Treasury Companies	Privatization Through Liquidation	Individual Sales
Number of enterprises			
less than 200 workers	308	950	24
between 200 and 500 workers	25	561	
more than 500 workers	68	243	
	215	146	
Total			
(percent of the number of state enterprises)	3.7	11.5	0.3

Source: Prywatyzacja przedsiebiorstw panstwowych, 1992.

Table A.6
Small Privatization in Russia, end of 1992

	Total enterprises	Commercialized	Percent	Privatized	Percent
Russia total	320,953	77,803	24	28,245	9
City of Moscow	16,220	9,600	59	8,355	51
Nizhny Novgorod	2,911	2,618	90	1,008	34
St. Petersburg	8,926	2,804	31	1,912	21
Krasnodar	13,793	3,192	23	1,003	14
Irkutsk	6,447	1,578	24	307	4
Tatarstan	6,940	69	1	4	0

Source: Russian State Property Management Committee, cited in B. Djelic and J. Sachs, "The Russian Mass Privatization Programme," manuscript, January 1993.

Table A.7
Privatization of Large Companies in Russia, End of 1992
(percentage distribution)

	Companies registered for commercialization	Privatization Plan completed		Registered as Joint Stock Companies	
		number	percent	number	percent
Russia total	6,329	1,263	20	637	10
City of Moscow	n.a.	–	–	–	–
Nizhny Novgorod	271	41	15	30	11
St. Petersburg	201	20	10	6	3
Krasnodar	171	46	27	44	26
Irkutsk	400	100	25	22	6
Tatarstan	n.a.	–	–	–	–

Source: Russian State Property Management Committee, cited in B. Djelic and J. Sachs, "The Russian Mass Privatization Programme," unpublished manuscript, January 1993.

Table A.8
Voucher Auctions in Russia, February 1993

Number of enterprises sold	723
Total charter capital of enterprises put on auction	40,933 million rubles
Total charter capital sold at auctions	10,305 million rubles
Total employment	834,000
Total number of privatization checks tendered	544,000
Weighted exchange rate	3.29 shares per privatization check

Source: Russian State Property Management Committee, cited in B. Djelic and J. Sachs, "The Russian Mass Privatization Programme," unpublished manuscript, January 1993; and B. Djelic, unpublished manuscript, March 9, 1993, Harvard Institute for International Development.

References

Aganbegyan, A. (1988). *The Economic Challenge of Perestroika*. Bloomington: Indiana University Press.
———. (1989). *Inside Perestroika: The Future of the Soviet Economy*. New York: Harper and Row.
Allen, M. (1990). "The Convertibility of the Rouble" (mimeo). Washington, D.C.: IMF.
———. (1974). "Towards Convertibility in Eastern Europe" (mimeo). Washington, D.C.: IMF.
Anikin, A. (1989). *USSR: Financial Crisis and International Monetary Policy*. Unpublished manuscript.
———. (1989a). *The USSR and the International Monetary System: Past Experience*. Unpublished manuscript.
Aslund, Anders. (1990). *Systemic Change in Eastern Europe and East-West Trade*. EFTA, Economic Affairs Department. Occasional Paper No. 31, June.
de Beus, Jos (1990). "The Interaction between a Free Market Economy and Liberal Democratic Politics." Paper prepared for a lecture at the University of Amsterdam, 4 October.
Bruno, Michael (1992). "Stabilization and Reform in Eastern Europe: A Preliminary Evaluation." Paper prepared for the International Monetary Fund, Washington, D.C., 5 February.
Dewar, M. (1951). *Soviet Trade with Eastern Europe 1945–1949*. London and New York: Royal Institute of International Affairs.

Diebold, W. (1952). *Trade and Payments in Western Europe: A Study in Economic Cooperation 1947–51*. New York: Harper. (Published for the Council on Foreign Relations).

Domar, Evsey D. (1989). *Capitalism, Socialism, and Serfdom. Essays*. Cambridge and New York: Cambridge University Press.

Dornbusch, R. (1992). *A Payment Union for the Former Soviet Union*. Unpublished manuscript, Massachusetts Institute of Technology.

Doronin, I. (1988). "Problemi sovershenstvovanija valutno-finansovich instrumentov." *Foreign Trade* (Moscow). No. 4 and No. 6.

Fischer, Stanley (1992). "Russia and the Soviet Union Then and Now." Paper prepared for the NBER Conference on "Transition in Eastern Europe," February.

Friedman, Milton, and Rose Friedman. (1980). *Free to Choose. A Personal Statement*. New York and London: Harcourt Brace Jovanovich.

Gold, J. (1971). *The Fund's Concept of Convertibility. IMF Pamphlet Series*, No. 14.

Hayek, Friedrich von (1946). *The Road to Serfdom*. London: Routledge.

Held, Joseph, ed. (1992). *The Columbia History of Eastern Europe in the Twentieth Century*. New York: Columbia University Press.

Hicks, John (1986 [1969]). *A Theory of Economic History*. Oxford: Clarendon Press.

Holzman, F. (1978). "CMEA's Hard Currency Deficits and Rouble Convertibility." In Nita G. M. Watts (ed.), *Economic Relations between East and West*. London: Macmillan.

Kaplan, J., and Schleiminger, G. (1989). *The European Payments Union: Financial Diplomacy in the 1950s*. Oxford: Oxford University Press.

Katz, S. (1991). "Transition." Washington, D.C.: The World Bank.

Keynes, J. M. (1963). *Essays in Persuasion*. New York: Norton Library.

———. (1988 [1919]). *The Economic Consequences of the Peace*. Middlesex, England: Penguin Books.

Klaus, Vaclav. "Transition—An Insider's View." *Problems of Communism* 41, No. 1–2 (1992): 73–75, 73.

Konstantinov, J. (1989). "Konvertiruemost rublja: konzeptualnii podhod." *Voprosi Ekonomiki*, No. 9, pp. 33–40.

Kornai, J. (1990). *The Road to a Free Economy: Shifting from a Socialist System: The Case of Hungary*. Unpublished manuscript, Cambridge, Mass.

———. (1992). *The Socialist System: The Political Economy of Communism*. Princeton, N.J.: Princeton University Press.

Krueger, A. (1978). *Liberalization Attempts and Consequences*. Cambridge, Mass.: Ballinger.

Kuznetsov, K. (1988). "Byt li u nas valutnimi rinki." *Ekonomicheskaja Gazeta* (Moscow), No. 26:21.

Lipton, David, and Sachs, Jeffrey (1992). "Prospects for Russia's Economic Reforms." September 16. Unpublished manuscript, Harvard University.

McKinnon, Ronald (1991). *The Order of Economic Liberalization: Financial Control in Transition to a Market Economy.* Baltimore: Johns Hopkins University Press.

Okun, Arthur M. (1975). *Equality and Efficiency: The Big Tradeoff.* Washington, D.C.: Brookings Institution.

Putnam, Robert D. (1993). "Social Capital and Public Affairs." *The American Prospect*, No. 13 (Spring): 1–8.

Radio Free Europe/Radio Liberty. (1992). RFE/RL Research Report, Vol. 1, No. 28 (10 July 1992).

———. (1992). RFE/RL Research Report, Vol. 1, No. 32 (14 August 1992).

Rosefielde, Steven (1991). *Markets and the Failure of Radical Soviet Economic Reforms.* Unpublished manuscript.

Sachs, J. (1990). "What Is to be Done?" *The Economist*, 13 January 1990, pp. 21–26.

———. (1990a). "Charting Poland's Economic Rebirth." *Challenge* (January-February): 22–30.

Sachs, J., and Lipton, D. (1989). *Exchange Rate Convertibility.* Unpublished manuscript, Washington, D.C.

Samuelson, Paul, and Nordhaus, William D. (1989). *Economics*, 13th ed. New York: McGraw-Hill.

Schumpeter, Joseph A. (1942, 1947). *Capitalism, Socialism and Democracy.* New York and London: Harper and Row.

Seidl, C., and W. Stolper, eds. (1985). *Joseph A. Schumpeter Aufsätze zur Wirtschaftspolitik.* Tübingen: J.C.B. Mohr.

van Brabant, J. M. (1989). "Regional Integration, Economic Reform and Convertibility in Eastern Europe." *Jahrbuch der Wirtschaft Osteuropas*, Band 13/1: 44–81.

Wiles, P. (1973). "On Purely Financial Convertibility." In Yves Laulan, ed., *Banking, Money and Credit in Eastern Europe.* Brussels: NATO Directorate, pp. 119–125.

Wolf, Charles, Jr. (1991). "Getting to Market." Santa Monica, Calif.: Rand Corporation, July.

Zloch-Christy, Iliana (1988). *Debt Problems of Eastern Europe.* New York and Cambridge: Cambridge University Press.

———. (1990). "Some Issues on the Convertibility of the Eastern European Currencies." Research study prepared for the U.N. Economic Commission for Europe, Geneva.

———. (1991). *East-West Financial Relations: Current Problems and Future Prospects.* Cambridge: Cambridge University Press.

Index

bureaucracy, 31, 32, 53

Canada, 105
Catholic Church, 74
capital account. *See* balance of
  payments
capital flight, 18
capital markets, international, 67
capitalism, 2, 4, 10, 14, 32
Central Bank, 51, 78, 92, 93, 94; of
  Bulgaria, 93
central planning, 5, 15; old style
  Soviet, 68
Central European Initiative (CEI),
  39
centrally planned: controls, 22;
  economies, xv, 71, 72, 83, 89,
  90; economic mechanism, 9;
  economic system, 44
Chechenya, 40
Chile, 48, 63, 69, 70, 75, 76, 93, 99
China, 53, 63, 64, 70, 77, 78
Chou En-lai, xv
Churchill, Winston, 99
CIS. *See* Commonwealth of Independent States
civil: culture, 61; servants, 55, 68,
  74; societies, 34, 35, 36, 37, 39,
  57, 61; war, 18
CMEA. *See* Council for Mutual
  Economic Assistance
Columbia, 93
commodity convertibility, 81, 85;
  inconvertibility, 90
Commonwealth of Independent
  States (CIS), xiv, 6, 13, 18, 44
communism, 2, 55; Soviet, 11
communist: Marxist or Soviet economies, 25; parties, 61; Party,
  xiv, 30, 33; rule, 2, 30; structures, 23, 29, 38, 41, 62, 113
communists, 11, 55, 60, 113

competition, 7, 48, 54; foreign, 48
constitutions, 21, 48
convertibility. *See* commodity
  convertibility; currency
  convertibility
corruption, 2, 54
Council for Mutual Economic
  Assistance (CMEA), 44, 45, 75,
  80, 106
country risk, 42
coup attempt, 29, 68
creditworthiness, 20
currency convertibility, xvii, 7, 48,
  79, 80, 81, 82, 84, 85, 86, 87, 88,
  89, 90, 91, 93, 94, 95, 96, 98,
  101, 102, 103, 104, 107, 108;
  policies, 48; inconvertibility, 85,
  86, 90, 97
current account, 48, 87, 102; deficit,
  19; transactions, 102
Czech lands, 2, 3
Czech republic, 9, 39, 40, 77; IMF,
  20; privatization, 52, 57
Czechoslovakia (former), xiv, 16,
  29, 38, 41, 44, 51, 56, 59, 73, 84,
  91, 93, 102

debt: domestic, 23; external, 19,
  44, 106; government, 48; large
  enterprise, 94; management, 14;
  relief (external), 50, 109
decentralization, 13, 54
decommunization, 40, 41
deflationary: adjustment policy,
  76; policies, 67; pressures, 43, 56
dekreti, 22
democracy, 1, 2, 31, 32, 33, 34, 35,
  36, 61, 63, 70, 76, 112; bourgeois, 2; constitutional, 11, 31;
  liberal, 36, 37, 113; Western-
  style, 48
democratization, xvii, 1, 55

About the Author

ILIANA ZLOCH-CHRISTY has been a consultant with the United Nations, International Monetary Fund, and other international organizations. She held faculty fellowships at the Department of Economics, the Center for European Studies, and Russian Research Center, all at Harvard University; at the Hoover Institution on War, Revolution, and Peace at Stanford University; and at St. Antony's College at Oxford University, U.K. She holds a Ph.D. in economics from the University of Vienna, Austria, and has worked as a research fellow at the Bulgarian Academy of Sciences. Dr. Zloch-Christy has travelled extensively in Eastern Europe, and is fluent in many languages including Bulgarian, German, English, and Russian.